ROCK COACH

A Practical Guide for Teaching Rock Bands in Schools

Steve Giddings

Steve's Music Room
PUBLISHING

ISBN: 0-9959155-0-4
ISBN-13: 978-0-9959155-0-3

Steve's Music Room Publishing
Prince Edward Island
Canada

www.stevesmusicroom.com

This book is dedicated to all the music teachers who want to be better music educators or need some inspiration to cater to more kids at their schools, and to all the kids in those schools who need an outlet for their music making.

Table of Contents

ACKNOWLEDGEMENTS I would like to thank Karri, my editor, who is not only amazing with words but a wonderful music educator in her own right. She was able to take what I was thinking and put it exactly to how I was trying to say it. Her guidance at every step of this publishing project was amazing. I would also like to thank Natasha for her coaching in the design of the book cover. She was able to refine my designs to precisely what I was looking for. I would never have started publishing my writing in the first place if it wasn't for Dr. June Countryman. Her inspiration helped me to publish my first article in the Canadian Music Educator Journal during my undergraduate work at UPEI. Of course, I would like to thank my fantastic wife, Jenn, for supporting me throughout this endeavor even during the most stressful parts of the publishing process. I would also like to thank my friends and family for their encouragement and support throughout this project.

Introduction

Imagine you are at a rock concert. You're listening to the tight groove, the excellent musicianship, the shredding solos. Now, imagine those musicians you are listening to are kids—your students. These current and potential rock musicians already exist in your school—yes, even in your elementary school—but may not be being given the opportunity to showcase or hone their musicianship in the school music program. Budding young rock musicians must learn their craft outside of school, and many others never have the opportunity to realize their potential because the music they truly enjoy and connect with is not represented in their schools' music programs. In my home province of Prince Edward Island, Canada, there is a growing movement of music teachers who are embracing the school rock ensemble as a way to complement their programs and engage kids in music in a completely different way. This book aims to change the perception of teaching rock music in schools and provide more opportunities for student success in music. It is intended to provide the motivation and the practical tools to help any music teacher build a successful rock ensemble in their school, no matter their level of experience, in a practical way.

Who Is This Book For?

In purchasing this book, it is clear that you have a passion for music education, and are craving something new and exciting. You want to start a rock group at your school but are not sure how to do it, or maybe you have rock bands at your school and want a few tips. Perhaps you are a music education student in university or maybe you are that teacher looking for a bit of inspiration. Maybe your program is small or dwindling and you are looking for additional ways to engage students further and to promote your program.

For the purposes of this book, I will assume that the teachers reading this possess a music degree or are working toward a music degree and have a basic understanding of the rudiments of music theory. This means you should understand how to read traditional music notation and have an understanding of basic chord harmony. Throughout this book I will share many of my own techniques and resources with you so that you feel comfortable coaching a successful rock ensemble and are aware of the unique practices pertaining to this genre of music. While I am currently working with elementary rock ensembles, secondary educators will find plenty of material to work with here, including the framework for an entire rock ensemble high school course (see Chapter 10). Whether you teach in an elementary or a secondary setting, if you are interested in bringing rock ensembles into your music program, this book is exactly what you are looking for.

Rock Bands in the Schools: How I Got Here*

Rock music is typically considered to be something that adults do. When a group of elementary school students perform music that is considered to be exclusive to adult performers, audiences are automatically impressed without really knowing why! When I was a music education major at the University of Prince Edward Island, I envisioned a complete school music program that included bands, orchestras, choirs, jazz bands and yes, rock bands. I published an article in the Spring 2008 issue of *Canadian Music Educator* during my time at university called "Popular Music Education: A Different Type of Musicianship." The article was essentially an outline and philosophy behind a course I had designed which was fully intended to be offered exclusively in a high school setting (see Chapter 10 for more details). Having focused my teacher education in Grades 7–12 instrumental music, I envisioned myself leading just such a

---

* Portions of this section were previously published in the Canadian Music Educator Journal volume 52, issue 2, pp. 33–36.
† Portions of this section were previously published in the Canadian Music Educator Journal

program when I graduated. Once my job search began, I soon found out that I should be ready to take whatever I could get. I ended up landing a miniscule gig teaching music at a small Prince Edward Island primary school of 53 students. Despite my reservations, as the year went on I began to enjoy teaching younger children and started to realize what they were actually capable of. Being very passionate about having popular music in schools, I decided to try starting a rock band with a Grade 4 class of 11 students. I brought in all of my own equipment including a drum set, two old beater electric guitars, a bass and a couple of small amps I had lying around my parent's basement. None of these children had any background in any of these ins-truments but I still decided it would be a good idea. I held auditions to see which instrument each student would be most successful at. When the band was chosen, all of the students had a role to play in it. There were two guitar players, one bass player, one drummer, two keyboard players and five singers. The song that they ended up learning was "You Really Got Me" by The Kinks. It took them a couple of months to get it, but they successfully pulled it off in the spring concert and boy, were they excited.

That tiny school closed its doors for good in 2009 and now I am at a much bigger school of 400 plus students from Kindergarten to Grade 6. Over a two day span I get to see all of these young musicians pass through my music classroom. When I was interviewed for the job I was asked if I had any experience teaching a rock band at this level, which surprised me because I thought I was the only person doing it at the time! As it turned out, the previous teacher had begun to take three or four students and form a small rock group to showcase a few different talents in the school. When I began in September of that year, I held auditions for the rock band and opened it to guitar players, keyboard players, singers, and drummers. The requirements, like the course I had designed for high school, were that they had to have been playing their instrument for at least two years or have been taking lessons on that instrument. When this band was chosen there were two vocalists, three guitar players, two dru-mmers and a keyboard player. All of these students were in Grade 6 except for the drummers. One of the drummers, who I ended up teaching private drum lessons to for the year, was in Grade 3 and the other was in Grade 4. As I had expected, no bass players auditioned so I had the guitar players switch around between bass and guitar depending on the song. They called themselves PennyBack and from there I began with lesson one from my high school course, and using the binder I had made as a resource throughout the year. After my amazing experience with these students during my first year at that school, I wrote a sequel article to the one written during my undergrad called "Popular Music Education: A Different Type of Musicianship, the Follow-up," which was published in the Winter 2010 issue of the *Canadian Music Educator Journal.* It highlights the experiences I had and what I had learned over the first year there about teaching rock music to a group of elementary school students and the successes that came from it. Now, the school owns enough instruments to run the program well and has expanded to two bands who perform at a yearly rock concert I developed called the PEI Schools of Rock Showcase featuring rock music performed by PEI students aged 8 to 18 from around the province. In 2017, the show featured 13 school rock ensembles from around the Island—the movement is growing!

Chapter 1: Why Rock Bands?

Rock music focuses on different skills and is learned differently than more traditional styles of music. In my experience performing rock music on various instruments, different skills are given greater emphasis. For example, reading and understanding written music are not as important or even expected as much as a good ear and the ability to *fake it*. For the most part, reading and understanding written music is not needed to be a world class rock musician. Creativity occurs much more organically and naturally with this style of music as well. You would be hard pressed to come across a rock musician that hasn't at least dabbled in composing their own music either on their own or in a group (discussed in Chapter 5). If you are reading this book, you are already partly convinced that rock bands are a viable option in music education but if you need further reaffirmation, or perhaps you need to convince a colleague or administrator, here it is:

ROCK BAND...

Engages Those Students Who Would Not Normally be Involved in Any Other Music Activity in School

Throughout my time coaching rock bands at my school, there is one aspect about their group composition that stands out. Many—if not most—of the students involved in these rock ensembles are not engaged in any other extracurricular ensemble. What is particularly striking about this is that boys are more likely to be hooked on playing music if this type of ensemble is offered. For anyone who has spent any period of time teaching in public schools, engaging boys in anything school related can generally be quite a challenge. Rock bands provide equal opportunity for both boys and girls to be successful in music.

Acts as an Enrichment Program for Gifted Children

We all have them, those high achieving students that do well in all areas at school. There is just one problem—they aren't being challenged. A rock band can easily provide that challenge students are looking for. I have had a student in the past that would be considered a model student who excelled in every aspect of school and life. She also happened to be taking piano lessons outside of school. Any concepts or skills we learned in music class were beneath her. She was always one step ahead of me and many times seemed to understand music better than I did! She became a piano/keyboard player in the band when she was in Grade 4 but easily could have made it in before that if auditions were available to students in Grade 3. I challenged her and picked very keyboard and piano-heavy tunes for her to play that year. There were times where we would do a tune that required her to play two separate keyboards at a time, while switching sounds on both without missing a beat. It was a challenge that she craved, and she loved it.

Effectively Engages Students in Learning

There have been at least two students that jump out to me as easily being poster children for music education. They found their niche through the rock band at school. Other ensembles can do this but these kids never found their place in any other

> The best predictor of future success is past success—any success.

school activity—curricular or extracurricular. At least one of them went from completely un-engaged in school with behaviour problems to very polite and engaged due to his membership in the rock band at school. The best predictor of future success is past success—any success.[1] You can read about this student in my article titled "Why Our Work Matters," which can be found on my website (www.stevesmusicroom.com) under the publications section or in the Fall 2016 issue of the *Canadian Music Educator Journal* released quarterly by the Canadian Music Educators' Association.

Is More Relevant to Students (And Audiences)

Rock music is everywhere. When we turn on the radio, it's there; when we go to a sporting event, it's there; when we go a concert, it's there. We can't get away from it and because of this, students *know* rock music even if they don't realize they do. It's hardwired into all of our DNA. When we think of music in schools, the last type of music that comes to mind is rock music. Should it not be one of the first? Think of it this way: A typical physical education program in a school includes exposure to many different sports. Most of these sports are easily found outside of school and most are part of our society. Most activities and sports they play in school are extremely relevant and relate perfectly to personal enjoyment *outside* of school. For example, hockey, at least in Canada, is considered our national winter sport and is engrained into our society. It is played in school, and out of school. A physical education program that does not include *at least* floor hockey would be considered blasphemous. Think of dodgeball—there are no or *very few* professional leagues for dodgeball and the only place it really exists is in schools. The reason recreational leagues exist now outside of school is because we *all* had it *in* school. Now, relate this to a music program—replace the word "Hockey" with the words "Rock Band" and the word "Dodgeball" with "Concert Band." If we exclude music that is regularly played outside of school, how is school music relevant for students? With the exception of army bands, there are no or *very few* professional concert bands outside of school and the only reason community bands exist is because they did it in school. So not only are rock bands extremely familiar to students, they directly relate to rock music outside of school. By including it in our school music programs, we ready our students to better compete in the real world of music making after they graduate. On that same wavelength, student rock bands can connect with an audience better than other ensembles can. Audiences love to hear music they know. This is one of the main reasons cover bands do so well and the starving musician persona that plagues original bands exists.

Naturally Focuses on Creativity, Memory, and By-Ear-Learning[†]

Rock music is, by nature, creative. Having played in many types of ensembles throughout my career, I never feel more creative than when I play rock music. There are no written parts, no chord charts, no score, and no conductor.[2] There are many opportunities for writing your own music and improvising solos. Keep in mind, students don't have to create entire songs to be creative. They can simply present form and arrangement ideas within a song; I call these musical choices. I have had students make a musical choice to change the bass line at the end of "Eye of the Tiger" because they felt it sounded better that way. They were right, it did, and it didn't change the integrity of the song. Sometimes, students at my school have to make creative musical choices just to finish a song. Some extended outros (opposite of an intro) are often impossible to recreate because they were created in the studio or they

> Having played in many types of ensembles throughout my career, I never feel more creative than when I play rock music.

just don't sound right in a live setting, and it is always impossible to recreate a live fade out. Instead of worrying about how to do it, the students and I figure out a way to end the song that makes sense. Essentially, they create their own ending for most songs that they play. These creative opportunities present themselves regularly when teaching rock music and students can do this quite naturally and with little thought or hesitation. Later on in this book I examine students' inherent creativity and suggest ways to get students writing their own music.

When I perform with The Sidewalks (my own original band) or with other rock ensembles everything is performed by memory, forcing the musicians to listen to each other more and create a tight sense of groove. Composing songs greatly helps in developing this skill because the composition literally becomes a part of you. I have had students in the rock bands over the years who had developed such advanced memory skills that they would only need to run a tune once or twice to get it.

Many if not all of the students in my school rock bands over the years developed tremendous aural skills that any university music student would be envious of. One of

---

[†] Portions of this section were previously published in the Canadian Music Educator Journal volume 55, issue 2, pp. 44–46.

the piano players that I had could read music very well but had very little need to implement that skill with the band. Her ear, by Grade 6, had become so developed that she could listen to something once and play it back. I have had many other instrumentalists over the years that developed ears like this. This is mostly due to the fact that rock music is naturally learned by ear or by imitation. In Chapter 6, I write about learning rock music authentically which includes by-ear-learning and the research of Dr. Lucy Green.

Provides Opportunities for Expansion‡

The fact is that this type of music gets more students interested in your program and wanting to participate in extracurricular activities. During my spring concerts, all of the other students from Grades 4–6 did choreographed dances to a few of the songs that the bands had played. The dancing helped to involve more of the school than just those involved with a class song, choir, rock band, or guitar club. This is another way that the band helps to involve more students in the music program in general. I examine this further in Chapter 11. An extracurricular guitar club can be a much less stressful way of implementing rock music into your program than a rock ensemble if you need a place to start. In time, the guitar club can act as a feeder program for the rock band, which over time may grow into multiple ensembles. Later, in Chapter 10, I will give effective ways in which to incorporate rock ensembles into your classroom to hook more students and not just have rock band as an extracurricular ensemble.

Develops Musical Independence More Effectively Than Other Ensembles

By nature, rock bands do not need a conductor. This forces these musicians to listen to each other and play as an ensemble. Sure, I've had to remind my bands a few times to listen to each other and pay attention, but if a teacher can resist the overwhelming urge to play with or conduct their students, then students begin to rely on each other more and develop their ability to play with other musicians much quicker and much more effectively. During this past year's spring concert I may have given each band three or four visual cues and then sat back at the sound board and let

‡ Portions of these two sections (Provides Opportunities for Expansion and Develops Musical Independence More Effectively Than Other Ensembles) were previously published in the Canadian Music Educator Journal volume 52, issue 2, pp. 33–36.

them do all of the music on their own. Essentially, if they are being coached well, eventually they won't need you.

Works Really Well with Small Class Sizes

Although regular class sizes are expanding, many times in intermediate or high schools where music is not mandatory, class sizes are smaller or are dwindling. Wind bands need large numbers of students to be effective. Rock bands will work with as little as four students and as many as 30. The larger classes would be divided into smaller ensembles that would stay together for the year or rotate members but still keep the small ensembles intact.

Is Less Expensive Than Other Ensembles

Due to the rate at which instruments such as electric guitars, drums, and keyboards are produced, they are much less expensive than many other types of instruments. Much of the time, chances are pretty good that there are people in the community that will donate them to your school. Chapter 3 discusses ways you can acquire these instruments and all the gear that you will need to be successful with it.

Breeds Instrument Versatility

I don't know a lot of rock musicians who only play one instrument in the band. It is very common for rock musicians to be able to play multiple instruments, or even every instrument in the rock band quite well. This is because rock musicians learn based on interest and will naturally gravitate to learning new instruments because they are not forced to play only one for an extended period of time. A broader discussion on how rock musicians learn is in Chapter 6. A prime example of this in the rock music world is Dave Grohl who played drums in the grunge band Nirvana, as well as other bands like Queens of the Stone Age but is also guitar and lead vocalist for the band Foo Fighters. The Beatles were also famous for playing multiple instruments on their studio albums. I have had groups in the past that were primarily singers but wanted to play keyboards in a particular song and another instance where a singer had to fill in for a guitar player in a concert. Their skill on both was strong enough that they were able to do both. We have even attempted having everyone in the band switch to a new instrument for one song. Chapter 10 discusses how this practice may look in a school setting.

Is a Lot of Fun to Coach

This is pretty self-explanatory. Most times, the rock band rehearsals are my favourite parts of the week. The students will have a lot of fun and so will you!

CHAPTER 2

Chapter 2: How do I do That?!

You might be thinking, "this is all well and good, but how do *I* do this? I mean, I have no training in these instruments, nor in this genre of music. How can a classically trained trombonist like me possibly teach anything other than concert band?" Easy—I did it. I am a classically trained trombonist who learned guitar for the sole reason of teaching elementary school. I didn't learn it overnight and I wasn't very good at first but since I was forced to play it with the kids, I ended up learning pretty quickly. I still wouldn't call myself a guitar player but I could hold my own playing along with somebody else. This brings me to the first of three key ways in which *you* can begin to coach a rock band at your school...

Have an Open Mind

Do not be afraid to learn with your students. When you learn with your students you are keeping one step ahead of them or even in step with them and in the process you are learning how to play and how to *teach* the instrument. In doing this, you will learn in the way rock musicians naturally learn their instruments. See Chapter 6 for more on informal learning processes. In this way, you are more like your students than you want to believe. They learn best when they teach somebody else too. It is exactly like Lev Vygotsky's theory of the zones of proximal development.

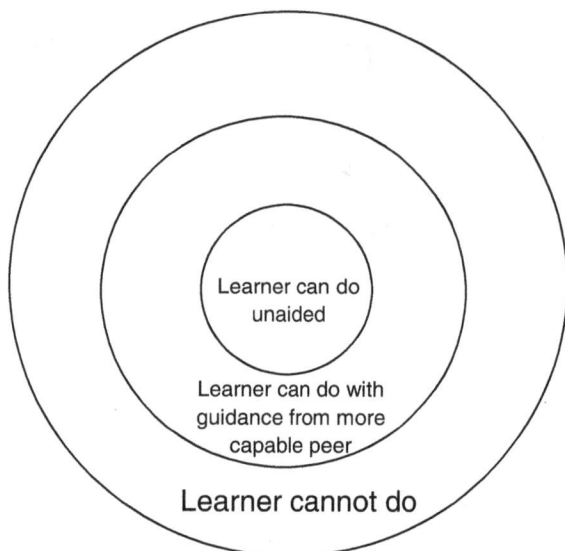

The zones of proximal development (ZDP) is "the distance between the actual developmental level as determined by independent problem solving and the level of potential development as determined through problem solving under adult guidance, or in collaboration with more capable peers."[3] From this definition, the teacher would be considered the more capable peer or the *Coach.* You could also do as the theory suggests and have the students teach each other. This also plays into the research of Lucy Green who suggests that the teacher should be the *Facilitator* and let the students do most of the teaching. Having the students be in charge will take longer but will take some of the pressure off you as the teacher. Lucy Green's research as well as Vygotsky's zones leads into my next point.

> Do not be afraid to learn with your students.

Think of Yourself as a Coach or Facilitator

Simply thinking about yourself as a coach or facilitator can greatly decrease the pressure on you and help to make learning *with* your students a very positive experience. The label of *Teacher* adds a level of stress that assumes you know everything and puts less onus on the learner. The term *Coach* implies that you are still in charge but are helping learners along to reach their goals while still giving them time to discover and learn from their mistakes. Think of a sports coach—a coach can still give homework, can still drill if need be, but in the end the onus is on the players to perform at the game without the coach, to learn from their mistakes and fix them on the fly. The term *Facilitator* is even more learner-centred still by almost completely removing the teacher from the picture and inserting them into a supervisory role while students discover much of the learning on their own.

My personal preference, as per the title of this book, is the term *Coach.* For me, it is the happy medium between too much control and not enough control over their learning. Fortunately, teaching rock music lends itself very well to thinking of yourself as a coach. This being said, I tend to flow between coach and facilitator depending on what students are doing or what is happening at the time. In certain situations while coaching a rock ensemble and teaching in general, more of a *Facilitator* approach is needed. An example of this would be when we are writing our own songs and creating new ideas. More about facilitating creative environments and songwriting activities will be discussed in Chapter 10. Here is a continuum that helps me to visualize each of these terms:

Leader   Teacher   Coach   Facilitator

|----------------------------|------------------------------------|-----------------------------------|

Teacher-centred   Learner-centred

At one time I would have used the term *Leader* synonymous with *Coach.* The more I thought about using this term to describe a teacher, however, I realized how negative of a term it can be in this context. The term *Leader* has a much less learner-centred implication and actually is almost, if not completely teacher-centred. It reminds me of old-school band leaders, conductors, and even world leaders, good and bad, who are deemed the all-knowing entities of their respective groups, accepting little if any student suggestion or feedback. Leaders lead, followers follow. This creates a creativity-hindering environment not conducive to teaching rock music.

I intentionally use the term *Learner* instead of student in many spots throughout this section and will continue to use it throughout this book. The term *Learner*, like the term *Facilitator* is a much less formal way to think of the word but also shifts the *teacher-student* relationship to *facilitator-learner. Student*, like the term *Leader* or *Teacher*, implies a very rigid type of learning and does not take into account the explorative aspect of learning in general.

Trust the Kids

We tend not to give learners enough credit. The fact is, you don't even need to know how to play the instruments because the kids will. The very first band that I coached at my current school had an amazing amount of skill, many of them could play their instruments better than I could. It was impressive. One learner in particular was completely self-taught and could play at a very advanced level. My YouTube Channel, which can be found on my website stevesmusicroom.com, has links to videos of that band performing. One of the most jaw dropping performances that band did was their rendition of "Dream On" by Aerosmith. What is even more amazing is that all that I did was tell them we were going to learn the song, and the kids did the rest. The only people in the band whose parts I helped to coach were the drummers.

I've also had learners who would be given the band CD for the year and have most of the songs learned the following week with zero coaching from me or anyone else. One of these students was a drummer who was going to extra physical education classes to improve his gross motor skills. I

> Your students, many times, know more than you think they do.

didn't even know about this until the end of the year because his motor issues seemed non-existent when playing the drums. This is why trusting the kids and why auditioning a variety of kids is important because you get to see students come out of the woodwork that would have been under the radar before. There is always someone in your school who can play something even a little bit. Your students, many times, know more than you think they do.

Professor Lucy Green is a British scholar who studies rock music, or *informal music* as she calls it, and its learning practices. Her research was instrumental in developing the *Musical Futures* program in much of Britain that teaches music by focussing on the learning practices of informal musicians. Her research took her into classrooms by actually working with students and teachers in real schools. Some of her work will be explored in a later chapter but teachers involved with this project "...unanimously agreed that "...using informal learning practices in the classroom has generally changed [their] approach to teaching for the better."[4] Teachers admitted that they were repeatedly surprised by their learners and that, in general, their expectations had been too low. They did not give learners enough credit for what they were actually capable of doing. Throughout this project, the teachers and the researcher realized that the main theme for the success of learners involved in this project was that of autonomy. Learners were given choice and freedom and therefore were pre-sented with the opportunity to discover learning on their own.

CHAPTER 3

Chapter 3: Equipment

So you're convinced, but what do you need? The equipment that most schools already have to facilitate this type of ensemble is minimal. New schools being built may be stocked with the appropriate equipment to run a rock band program, but realistically, many of us are not fortunate enough to have this luxury. As mentioned during the introduction, when I began teaching rock music, I took my own instruments from home for learners to use. I also realize that many do not have the good fortune of finding everything they need in their parent's basement so I compiled a list of equipment you will need or already have to get started.

Minimum Requirements

This is a list of the minimum equipment requirements to run a rock group at your school successfully. Any less than this will make it difficult to perform the music authentically.

What *most* schools already have:
- **A PA system with 5–8 channels**
- **2–3 vocal microphones with XLR cables**
- **A keyboard or electronic piano**
- **Keyboard amplifier**

Other equipment you will need but your school may not have:
- **At least one drum kit or pieces of a drum kit**
    - You can buy a beginner model kit for $500.00 and maybe even cheaper if you look around. Check your local classified ads for drum kits. Used drum kits are quite plentiful and relatively easy to find.
    - If you are looking for pieces, the minimum requirements would be a snare drum with stand, bass drum with a pedal, hi-hats with stand, and a crash cymbal with stand.
- **At least one guitar amplifier and one electric guitar**
    - Look at the **Mustang** series of **Fender** amps. They come in a range of sizes and are very versatile and well priced. They use an amplifier modelling system that imitates some of the best sounding and most iconic guitar amplifiers in the industry. They have a built in tuner and multiple effects. There are also programmable footswitches that go between two settings with the push of a button. Another guitar amplifier brand to look for is **Line 6**. Electric guitars will work if plugged into a PA system directly but you will not be able to get any of the effects or sounds that are so char-

AMPLIFIER

FOOTSWITCH

acteristic of the instrument so therefore is not recommended. This is why a guitar amplifier is a minimum requirement.

○ For guitars, look at the **Squier** line of **Fender** guitars. My school has two **Classic Vibes** and a **Jay Terser**. These instruments are decently priced and good quality.

○ Some students will likely already have a guitar and an amp if money is tight. Students owning their own instruments happens more commonly than you would think with this type of ensemble. My first two years teaching rock band, the guitarists brought their own guitars to school. This still happens often even though the school has their own instruments.

- **A bass and bass amp**
  ○ Keyboard amps can be used as bass amps. *Never* plug a bass guitar into a guitar amplifier. If your school has a keyboard amplifier with multiple inputs, it can double as a keyboard and bass amp at the same time.

NOTE: If your school does not have a bass amplifier or a keyboard amplifier, both instruments can plug directly into the PA.

- **3–5 patch cables and XLR cables**
  ○ Patch cables are male–male ¼" cables that connect any electronic instrument to its amplifier or to a mixer.

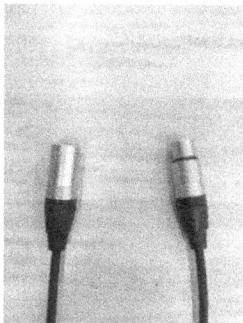

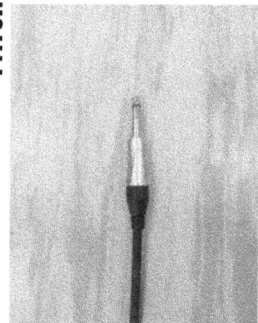

  ○ XLR cables are the three-pronged cables for microphones. As a minimum, you should have enough XLR cables for every microphone you plan to use. Many older speakers use a form of ¼" cables and some newer speakers have a hybrid capability that accept both ¼"and XLR inputs. If you have speakers that use XLR cables, make sure you have enough for those too.

This equipment is the bare minimum that you can get by with. I was able to do this for a couple of years successfully without any additional gear. We had a donated electric guitar and an old drum kit that the school had. If you have the means or the opportunity, the following is the recommended instrumentation and gear list that will help your groups sound better and easier to manage in a concert and rehearsal. Much of the following can also help your group sound more authentic as they would be closer to what the original band would have in a live setting.

Recommended Instrumentation

- Two or three 40 watt **amp modelling guitar amplifiers** with at least 12" speakers (1x12) in them and compatible footswitches. Built in tuners would be ideal.
- Enough **good quality guitars** for each amp.
- At least one **good quality bass guitar** and a 75–100 watt bass amplifier with at least a 12" speaker (1x12) or 15" speaker (1x15) in it. Built in tuners would be ideal. Also, bass amps with a built in DI (Direct Input) are recommended. The next section explains direct input.
- Two or three 60–88 key **keyboards or electronic pianos** with at least 60 different settings and effects. If the keyboards have a number of *synth leads* it makes them very versatile. Synth leads are the sounds primarily used for melodic material while *synth pads* are primarily used for background or chording material. Many keyboards can blend sounds to give you even more options.
- **Enough keyboard amplifiers for the number of keyboards your school has**. Life will be easier on stage if the amplifiers have a built-in DI (Direct Input).
- **A synthesizer or two.** Some of these would only be used for particular songs because many synthesizers have their own characteristic sounds depending on their brand name. For example, the song "Ghostbusters" by Ray Parker Jr. uses the specific trademarked sound of a Yamaha DX-7. You will likely be able to get sounds that pretty closely match any sound as long as you have a versatile keyboard so **actual synthesizers are not required** but are something to consider.
- One or two **five-piece drum kits with hardware**. A five-piece drum kit includes a bass drum, snare drum, small tom, medium tom, and floor tom. Hardware includes all cymbals and stands.

Currently, I have two acoustic drum kits and one electronic drum kit for my program. Normally, I will have up to two drummers playing at one time.

> NOTE: Electronic drum kits are versatile but can teach bad habits for more experienced players. Even the most expensive and highest quality electronic drum kits do not respond like acoustic kits. There are very few professional drummers that would choose an electronic drum kit over a good acoustic one. This being said, an electronic drum kit is great for private practice due to its volume and for teaching the basics of playing the instrument.

PA System

A basic PA system with a mixer and two speakers will do for rehearsal and in some performance situations. Performing, however, usually is done in a much bigger room which requires additional equipment. These items will make your bands sound better, will help your young musicians play better, and can really help your performances sound and look professional. You can still perform the music well and be successful with or without all of this equipment. Below is a list of basic sound equipment your school will need to make concerts easier and help to make your rock groups sound better, followed by detailed diagrams of a basic sound setup to get you started.

- **A mixer with at least 12 channels, with at least one monitor mix (AUX) that can be controlled on each channel**
  - You will need a separate channel for every instrument in your band. You can usually get away without micing the drums but in bigger halls you will need to mic the drums. If they are electric, you will need to put them through your mixer using a DI (Direct Input). An acoustic kit will at minimum need a bass drum mic and an overhead. Thus, if you are micing the drums, they need two separate channels per kit.

- o **Two common types of mixer configurations**:
  - **Powered**: With this configuration, only the mixer plugs into a wall outlet. The speakers get their power from the mixer. You know you have a powered mixer when it is heavy and has a wattage indicator on the back. This configuration is relatively easy to set up because you only need to plug in the mixer. The advantage to this type of setup is that you can set up virtually anywhere as long as you have one outlet.
  - **Unpowered**: With this configuration, there is no power provided from the mixer. These mixers can be much smaller than the powered ones but tend to have more options on each channel and more often have faders instead of knobs for volume control. With this configuration, **the speakers are powered** instead of the mixer. Using this configuration, all speakers, monitors, and the mixer will need their own power cables to plug in. Powered speakers will usually have an input to plug in a power cable and will be heavier than unpowered speakers because they have their own built in amplifiers. In a very rudimentary setup of a mixer with two speakers, you will need to plug in three pieces of equipment just for the PA. **You will know your speakers are powered if they have volume knobs on the back.**

- **At least two *main* speakers**
  - o This is usually shortened to just *mains*.
  - o These are the speakers that the audience will hear that plug into the mixer. If you have an unpowered mixer, you need powered speakers and vice versa.

- **Up to three monitors**
  - o Monitors are those speakers on the floor in front of the stage facing the performers. They help the musicians hear each other better due to the directionality of many speaker cabinets. For example, if a performer is behind the main speakers it can be very difficult for them to hear what is coming out of them so they need additional speakers facing them, called monitors, that have a separate mix from the mains. A separate mix means that the volume can be adjusted for those monitors separately from the main speakers. Some mixers have two or more monitor mixes. This means that each monitor can be adjusted separately from one another, customizing the monitor mix to each musician. This is a much more advanced setup.

- o Monitors work the same as speakers. If you have an unpowered mixer, you will need powered speakers to act as monitors. Any speaker can be a monitor.

- **At least two DI (Direct Input) boxes**
  - o You may remember a reference to DI boxes when discussing bass and keyboard amplifiers. You may only need one DI box if your keyboard and bass amplifiers are equipped with a built-in DI.
  - o **DI boxes have two main purposes**
    - One purpose is to change the signal going to the mixer so that all of the signals going to the board are the same. It takes the signal generated from a ¼"cable and converts it to XLR. The XLR cable is what goes to the mixer. XLR cables are grounded and give off virtually no hum. ¼" cables are not grounded and therefore generate a humming inter-ference. The longer they get and the more there are, the worse the hum.

    - The other is so the amplifier can act as a monitor for perfor-mance. Without a DI hooked into an amp, the sound from the instrument only goes out the main speakers with nothing coming back to the musician. The DI box lets your musicians control their *stage* volume separately from the main volume so that the person using the DI box can hear themselves during a performance. To do this, simply plug the instrument into the *input* hole on the DI with a ¼"cable and then the *in-thru* into the input on the amplifier. The XLR goes to the mixer and then the musician can control the keyboard amp like a monitor.

- **A 75–100 foot cable snake**
  - A cable snake is a piece of equipment that helps the person operating the sound board to be far away from the stage so that they can get a better gauge of the sound in the room and not be in the way of the performers.

CABLE SNAKE

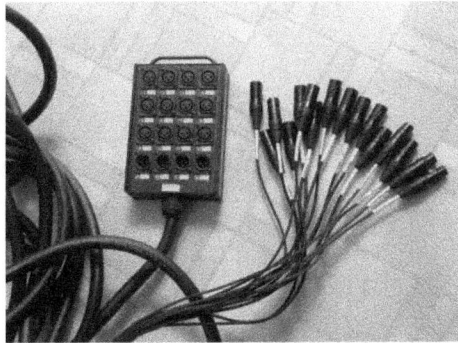

  - It has a box with XLR and ¼" channel inputs and speaker outputs on one end and male and female cable ends for the sound board/mixer at the other.
  - It really cleans up the performance area and instead of running 12–15 different wires across the room, you only run one.

NOTE: Think of the snake as a large extension cable for your mixer. The box is where all your microphones, instruments, and any speakers plug into and the male and female XLR ends plug into the mixer. Each cable is labelled and sometimes colour-coded.

The following diagram is designed to help you set up your first system using an un-powered mixer. **Unpowered mixers with powered speakers** are the best choice for a beginner because the speakers and mixers can be mix-and-matched without having to worry about electrical impedances or blowing a speaker cabinet.

Basic Setup with an Unpowered Mixer

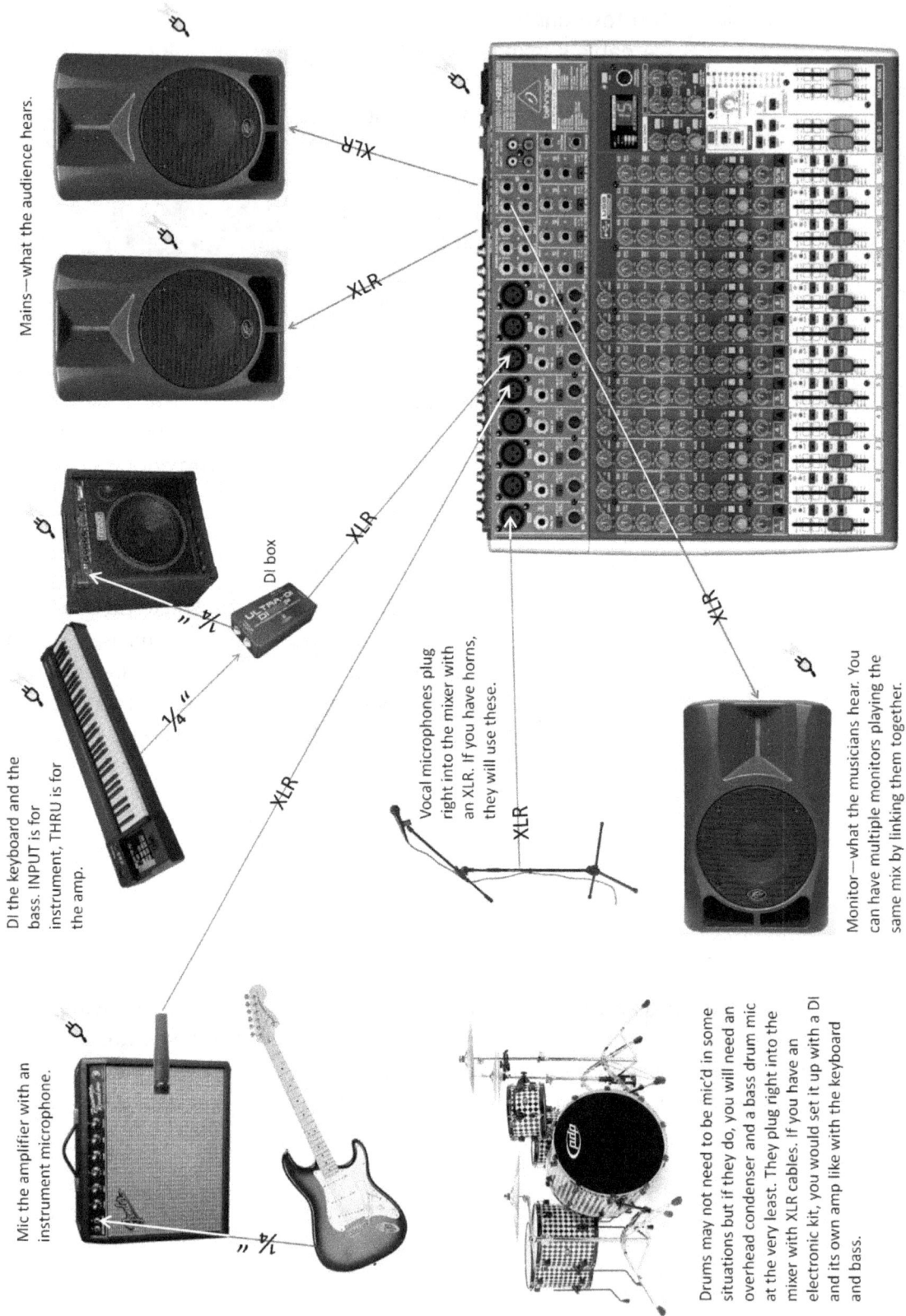

Mains—what the audience hears.

XLR

XLR

DI the keyboard and the bass. INPUT is for instrument, THRU is for the amp.

DI box

1/4"

1/4"

XLR

XLR

XLR

Vocal microphones plug right into the mixer with an XLR. If you have horns, they will use these.

XLR

Monitor—what the musicians hear. You can have multiple monitors playing the same mix by linking them together.

Mic the amplifier with an instrument microphone.

1/4"

Drums may not need to be mic'd in some situations but if they do, you will need an overhead condenser and a bass drum mic at the very least. They plug right into the mixer with XLR cables. If you have an electronic kit, you would set it up with a DI and its own amp like with the keyboard and bass.

NOTE: In the diagram on the previous page, you will need an adapter for the monitor mix. You will need a male XLR to male ¼"cable adapter for the mixer to the monitor. The ¼"end goes into the AUX SENDS, while the XLR end plugs right into your XLR cable that is going to your monitor.

Basic Mixer Info

The next diagram shows the basic inputs, outputs, and knobs you need to understand to run sound at your school successfully. Everything should work if you focus your attention on these:

INPUTS are where all the instruments plug into. GAIN refers to how much of the instrument's signal is let into the mixer.

AUX SENDS are controlled on each channel here.

VOLUME CONTROL for each channel. Each channel has a MUTE function.

AUX SENDS for your monitor.

VOLUME CONTROL for mains.

NOTE: AUX SENDS are your monitor mixes (what the musicians hear). You can control how much of each instrument is coming out of the monitor. The monitor mix will be different from the main mix (what the audience hears). Adjusting the AUX SENDS on each channel will *not* affect your main mix.

The best way to learn about how sound works is to just play with it. This is how I learned most of what I know about sound. As we know, most people learn better by doing than by being told what do to do. This being said, if you are the type of person who would like to know more by reading and referencing, here is a list of resources to check out to advance your skills:

- "Sound With Steve: Live and From Source Sound" presentation handout on stevesmusicroom.com. Check the lesson plans page under *Rock Band*. This gives a really good overview and diagrams on the basics of sound. A great place to start.

- *The Ultimate Live Sound Operator's Handbook 2nd Edition* by Bill Gibson (Music Pro Guides).

- *Handbook for Sound Engineers 4th Edition* by Glen Ballou.

- *Sound Reinforcement Handbook* by Gary Davis and Ralph Jones.

- *Sound Design Life: Build Your Career as a Sound Engineer* and *Master Your Craft: Sound System Tuning for Confidence and Consistency* both by Nathan Lively.

Acquiring Equipment

There is always the question of how to acquire the proper equipment. Unlike concert band instruments, sound equipment and rock instruments are plentiful and therefore cheaper and easier to find. Here are a few ways to acquire your equipment:

Take in Monetary Donations from Concerts

At my school, we accept monetary donations for our concerts. We find that people are very generous when donations are an option. If there is a set ticket price, you will get no more than that set price; if donations are a choice, people may give much more. In the program we include a statement about how the money from the concert will go back to purchase new instruments and equipment for the music department.

Classified Ad Websites

There are always good quality used instruments and sound equipment on classified ad sites like eBay or Kijiji. Many times, due to the fact that something such as an electric guitar is so common, finding a good quality used instrument should be quite easy. Facebook is becoming a great place to search for quality used instruments in your area too.

Ask For Instrument Donations

When I was starting up the guitar club at school, I put an ad in the local newspaper asking for used guitars in good condition or in need of minor repairs. The number of people with very nice guitars in their basements that had not been used for years was astonishing. In a two week period, we received 12 guitars from members of the community for *free*. We even got one electric guitar in barely used condition. Four or five of the guitars were playable right away and another couple needed minor repairs. At the time, a local luthier saw the ad in the paper and offered his services to repair the guitars that needed it. He was able to get four more guitars into playable condition and all he charged us for were materials. The same thing can easily happen with any of these other instruments in the rock band because everyone at one time wanted to be the next best drummer in the world but soon after purchasing a drum kit with the best of intentions, never played it again. This option would probably be the best place to start if money is tight.

Ask a Friend

Musicians and teachers are usually willing to help out other musicians and teachers. Ask your friends if they happen to have an instrument or piece of equipment they could part with or lend to the school during the year. Perhaps they will charge a small fee for the rental, perhaps they won't. From my experience, guitar players never own just one guitar, nor do they just own one amp. In most cases they have one they can part with or sell for a fair price. Knowing their instruments would be going to help the next generation of young musicians could be a nice selling feature to mention.

Rentals

Many music stores have rent-to-own options for most products or have very reasonable rental fees. Long & McQuade has locations all across Canada and has extremely good prices on rental equipment and a variety of payment options. Your province or state might have their own local music store with great prices.

CHAPTER 4 Chapter 4: Instrument Basics

So you have all of your equipment and instruments, what next? This chapter is all about the basics of how to play these instruments. These instruments include: guitar, drums, bass, piano/keyboard, and vocals. I also have included a broader discussion on the use of horns in rock bands. As mentioned, this type of music is learned primarily by ear and learned informally. It is also true that to learn a musical instrument properly, the learner (this includes you) needs to actually pick up the instrument. This means, once you have access to them, it is extremely important that you go back to play and experiment with some of the chords, patterns, and positions mentioned here using *actual* instruments. Some sections go into a little more depth than others but are, in essence, the very basic skills needed to be a successful rock coach. In the interest of learning these instruments in an informal way, like rock musicians do naturally, I intentionally did not get into specifics. After learning the basics from this book, apply your new skills to some songs you have been trying to learn or choose a song from the song list in the next chapter.

Guitar

Guitar, or electric guitar specifically, is the main instrument of the rock ensemble. Without the guitar, the music just doesn't quite sound the same. Bands usually have a lead guitarist who plays the solos or short licks and a rhythm guitarist who plays the chords and harmonic foundations. This section of the book will help you with the basics of the instrument and some advanced concepts as well.

Anatomy

Truss rod
cover plate

Nut

Frets

Head stock

Pickup selector switch

Body

Tuning pegs

Saddle

Inlays

Neck

Bridge

Pickups

Volume and
tone knobs

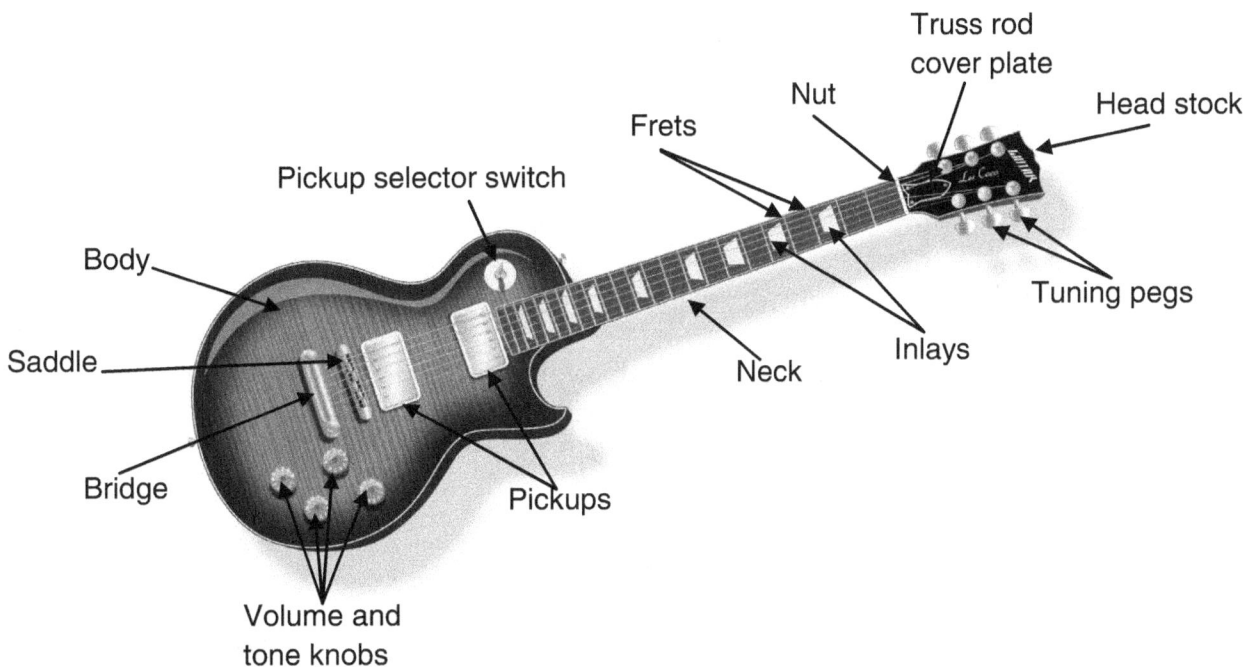

String Tuning

There are a number of tunings on a guitar. Standard tuning is the most common. Other common tunings are used in particular situations and styles. Those will be explained here. Using an electronic tuner is the most accurate and efficient way to tune guitars.

Standard Tuning

This is the tuning that around 85% of all rock songs use which means this tuning is the only one you will need to worry about for the most part:

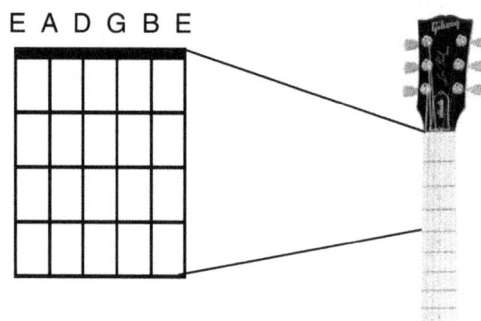

E A D G B E

In these diagrams, horizontal lines are the frets, vertical lines are the strings. The left-most string is the thickest (6th). The right-most is the thinnest (1st).

Drop Tuning

This type of tuning is typically used in heavy metal and similar styles of rock music. It facilitates one finger *power chords* (discussed later) and is characterized by dropping the 6th string by a full step. Below is *Drop D* tuning and other common drop tunings like *Drop C#* and *Drop C*.

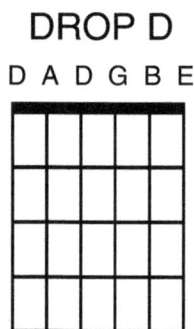

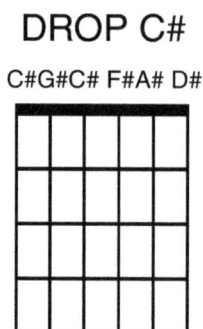

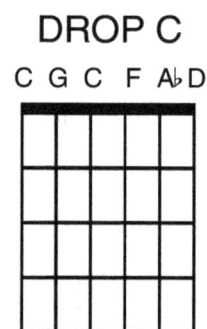

DROP D

D A D G B E

DROP C#

C#G#C# F#A# D#

DROP C

C G C F A♭ D

Any time the 6th string is dropped farther than one whole step, the other strings have to compensate to keep the intervals the same as in the *Drop D* example. For example, if we drop the 6th string down **two whole steps** (to C), the rest of the strings must compensate by being down tuned **one whole step**.

Down Tuning

This type of tuning is when **all strings are tuned down equally** by a ½ step or by a full step. Hard rock bands typically do this to make their songs sound heavier. Guns and Roses as well as Weezer are known for down tuning their guitars.

Other Tunings

Here are some other tunings that are not as common but used in different settings. Grab your guitar and a tuner and experiment with them.

DADGAD

D A D G A D

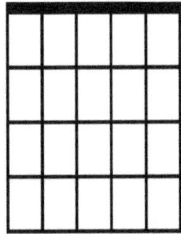

OPEN D

D A D F# A D

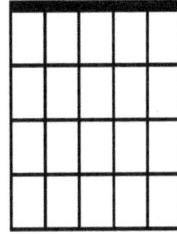

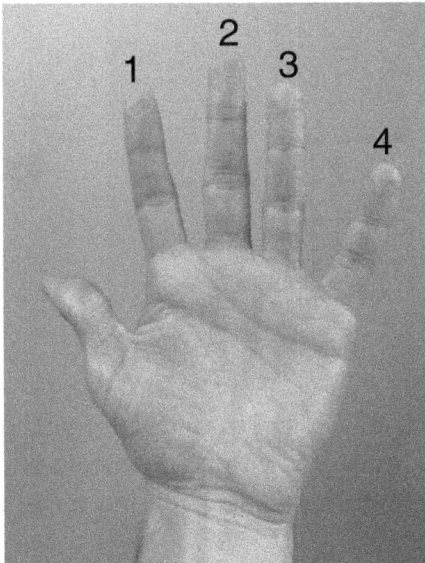

Fingering

Now that we have tuning out of the way, you need to know how your fingers are numbered in your left/chording hand when playing the instrument.

This picture to the left shows how the fingers are numbered. Notice, the thumb does not have a number. This is because it is not used for pressing down strings to form chords. Unless, of course, you are Jimi Hendrix, who used his thumb to form *barre chords* in many cases. Typically, though, it is not used.

The Main 7

The image to the right is a legend showing how to read chord fingering charts. Below are the seven chords that every guitar player should know. If you are only going to learn seven chords, it should be these:

How to Read a Guitar Fingering Chart

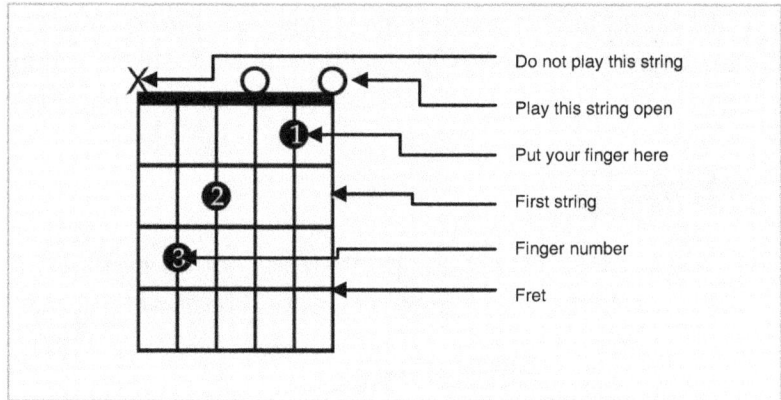

Do not play this string
Play this string open
Put your finger here
First string
Finger number
Fret

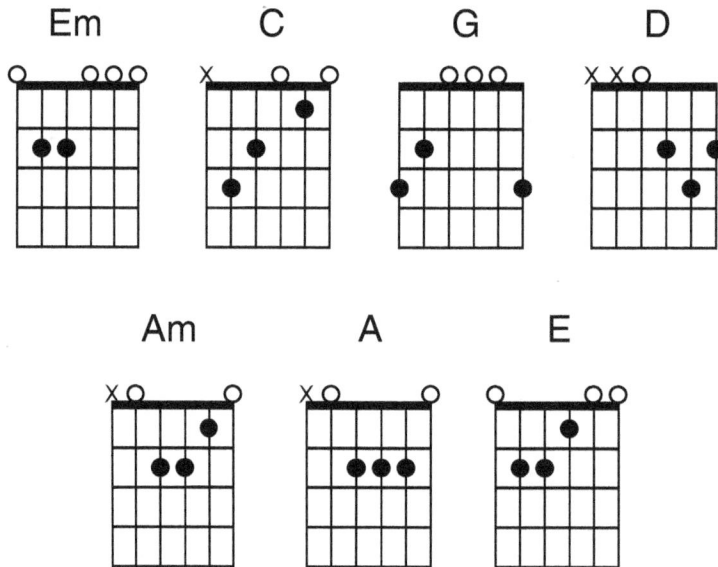

Em   C   G   D

Am   A   E

These are the most common chords that a guitar player will come across. If you or your learners are struggling with some of these forms, there are alternate ways to play nearly all of them that only require using one or two fingers at a time. In the case of Em, however, you don't even need any fingers.

These alternate or simplified versions of the seven main chords contain all of the notes for the triad so, in some cases, can actually be used instead of full chords. The timbre and voicing is just slightly different because the root note is not always the lowest sounding pitch. You can use these to work toward playing the fully voiced chord.

No-finger Em   One-finger C   One-finger G   D (no change)

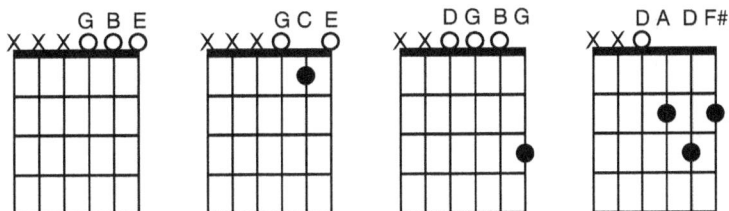

Two-finger Am   Two-finger A   One-finger E

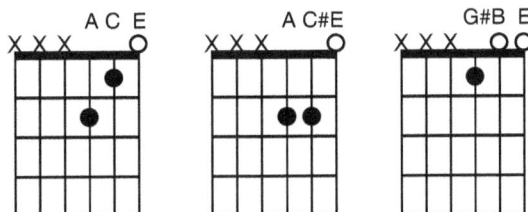

Moveable Chords: Barre Chords and Power Chords

This section teaches you about barre chords and power chords. These are moveable chord forms that have four basic shapes which can be seen below. First, here is a diagram of a guitar neck with the first eight frets of the fingerboard named for the 5th and 6th strings. I will explain why this is important in the next section.

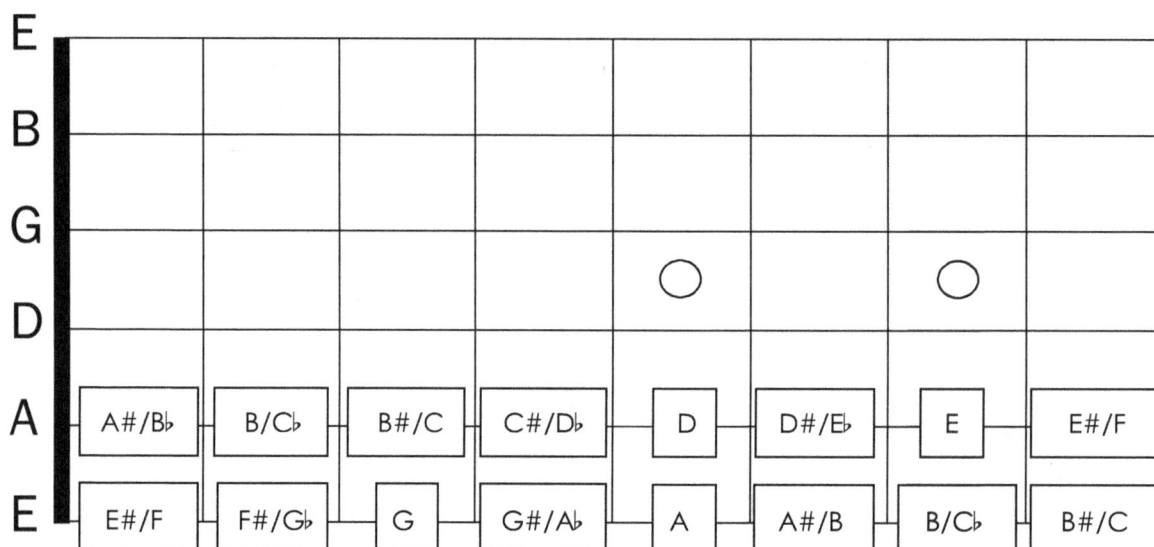

E

B

G

D

A	A#/B♭	B/C♭	B#/C	C#/D♭	D	D#/E♭	E	E#/F
E	E#/F	F#/G♭	G	G#/A♭	A	A#/B	B/C♭	B#/C

If a guitar player knows the root note, they can play any major or minor chord using this chart. The full barres and power chords are always formed from the root note on either the 5th or 6th strings. What makes these barre chords is that the first finger forms a barre by pressing down five or six strings all at one time making these chords quite a challenge to form for a beginner. For example, if you were looking for a C#m chord, you would form a 5th string *minor* barre form (see next page) starting on the 4th fret. There are also a few easier ways to barre that will be mentioned later.

Power chords are, essentially, barre chords without a 3rd. They consist of a 5th and an octave above the root. The best part is, no barre! They are very prominent in heavier styles of rock music. Also, what is convenient about power chords is that, in many cases, they can replace the full barre chord if your learners are not quite ready for barre chords. This is especially effective in distortion-heavy songs where the keyboard player will typically fill out the chords. If your learners are just being intro-duced to power chords, have them use their first finger only until they are more comfortable with the patterns in the song. Sometimes in a song that calls for power chords will still work if just the root notes are played. The letters and numbers above these fingering charts represent where the root (R), 3rd (3), and 5th (5) are in each shape.

Moveable Barre Chords

6th string *major* barre form

6th string *minor* barre form

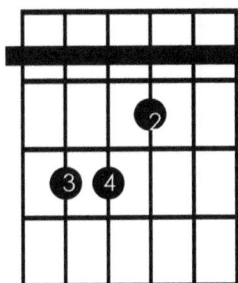

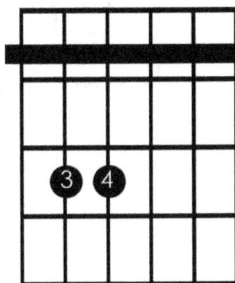

1st finger

5th string *major* barre form

5th string *minor* barre form

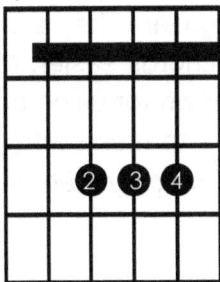

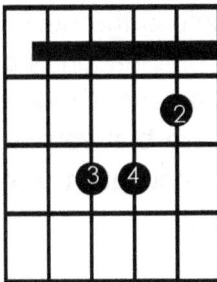

Power Chords

6th string power chord

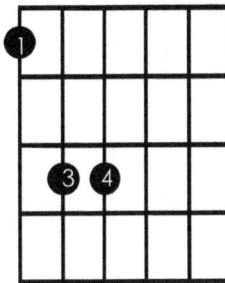

5th string power chord

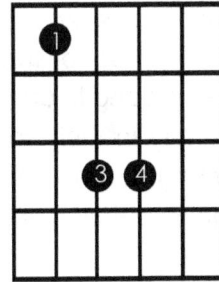

Simplified Barres

There are simplified ways to play barre chords. Imagine using your barre chords but only fingering and playing the 1st, 2nd, and 3rd strings. It is exactly the way that the *Main 7* are simplified. Experiment with this using your guitar.

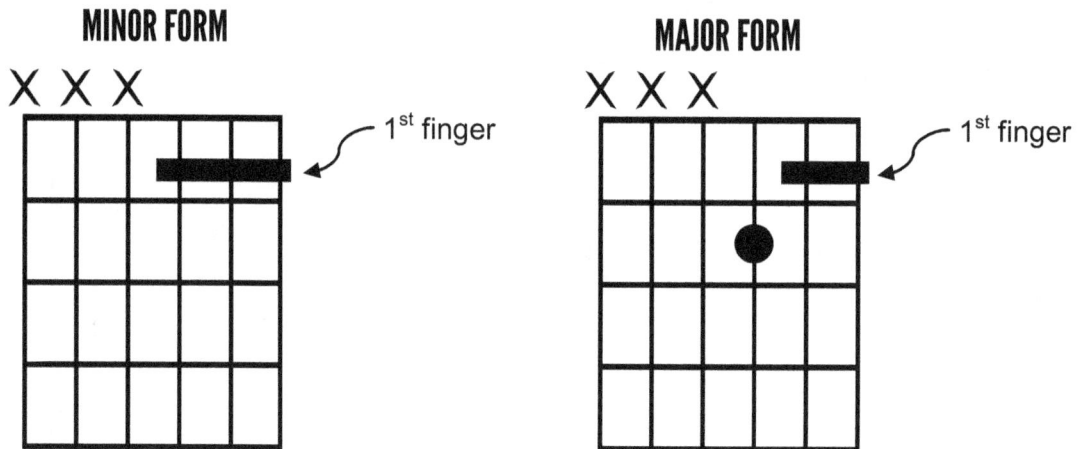

MINOR FORM

X X X

1st finger

MAJOR FORM

X X X

1st finger

Capos

Capos are spring loaded clamps that fit across the neck of the guitar. They are frequently used for transposing or making a combination of difficult chords easier. Many times a song is originally written to include a capo. Coldplay is known for using capos regularly in their songs. Think of it as a *barre* that you don't have to make with your first finger. Once the capo is on, that is the new guitar nut (see *Anatomy* diagram on page 33). Pick one up and experiment with it!

Scales

Playing guitar in a rock band isn't just about knowing your chords. Solos are just as important and therefore, scales are too. There are three basic scale patterns that every guitar player should know. They are the pentatonic *box* pattern, the blues *box* pattern, and the major scale pattern. For the sake of simplicity, I will start each pattern on the 5th fret. The large circles are the fingers and the numbers inside them are the finger numbers. The shaded circles are the tonic notes of the scale. It is extremely common for guitar players to know a plethora of scale patterns. This is because once a guitar player learns a pattern, it can easily be transposed into another key by moving the pattern up or down the neck. These are designed to get your learners started with scales and improvising solos.

For each of these patterns, you should start from the bottom, read left to right and then up.

Minor Pentatonic Box Pattern

This is the most popular scale pattern heard in rock music. It is extremely simple. It is clear by the shape of this pattern why it might be called the *box* pattern.

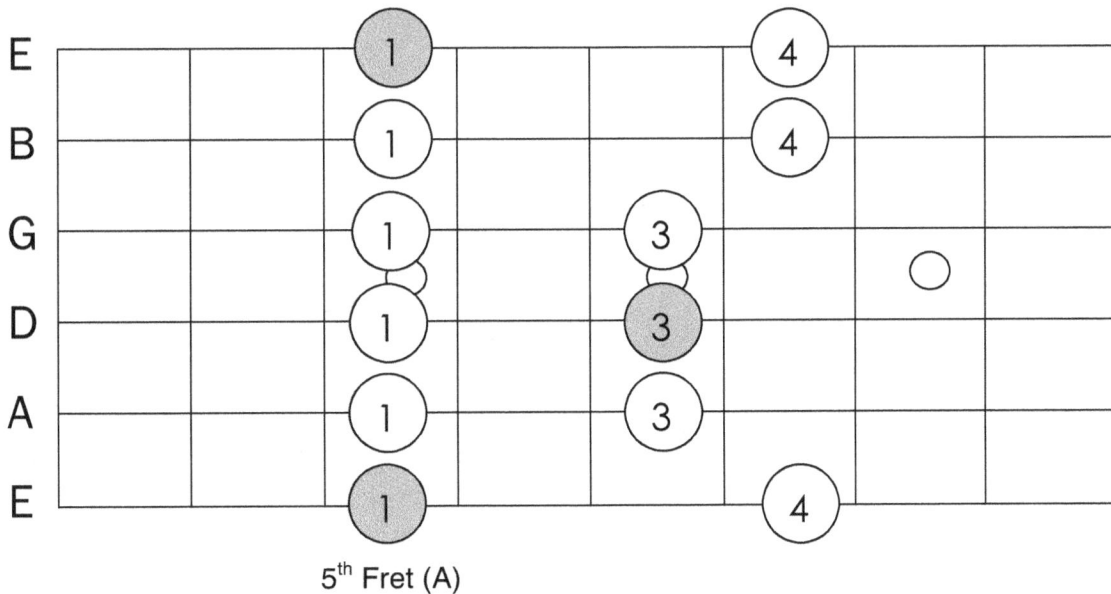

5th Fret (A)

Minor Blues Box Pattern

This is another extremely common scale pattern heard in rock music. There is only one note in the difference between the minor pentatonic scale and the blues scale. That note is called the *blue* note.

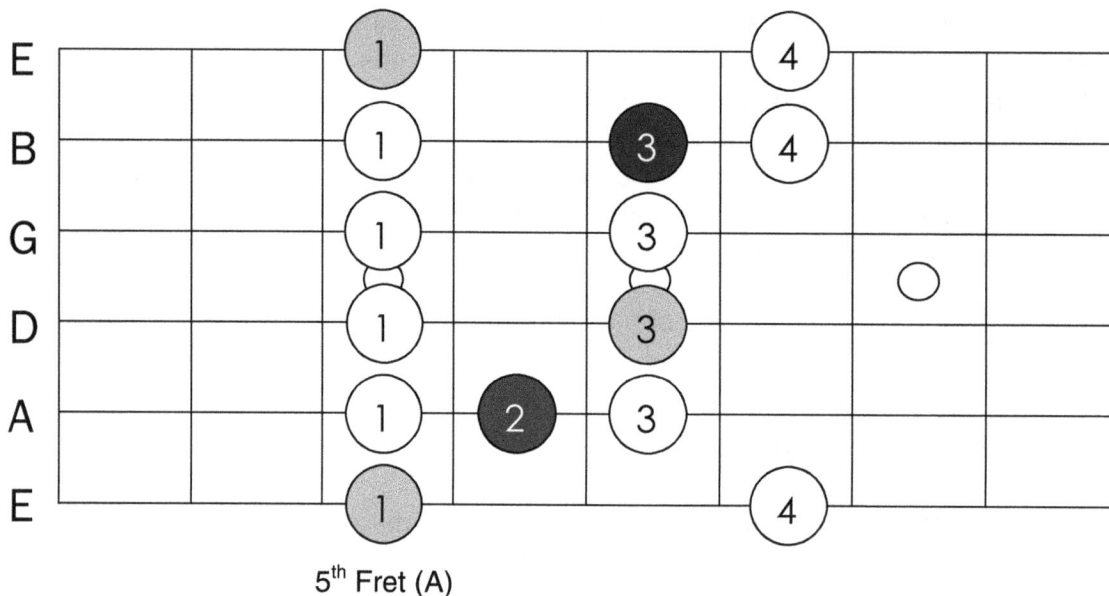

5th Fret (A)

Major Scale Pattern

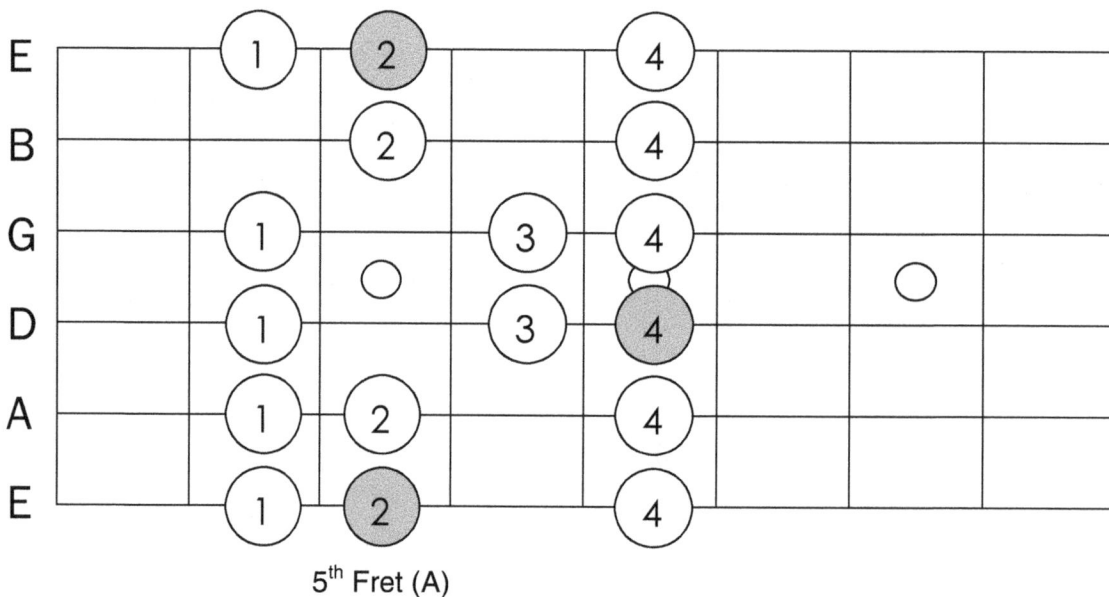

5th Fret (A)

Left-handed Guitars?

When coaching a group of learners through playing the guitar for the first time I always get one student, after showing them how to hold the instrument, exclaim "But Mr. Giddings, I'm left handed." Unlike every other Western instrument that I can think of, the guitar is the only instrument that has a flip-handed option. Jimi Hendrix became famous for not only his skill on the guitar but his rather unorthodox technique. He popularized the notion of a left-handed guitar because to solve the *perceived* problem, he turned his guitar around and restrung it for his right hand to play the chord forms.

Due to the nature of informal learning practices (discussed in Chapter 6), situations similar to Jimi Hendrix happen regularly. The particular learner, not having a person to teach them, just figures it out and many times what works for them is fine. If it sounds good and doesn't hurt, then there is absolutely no problem with it. Another prime example of this informal learning style is Jeff Healey. But instead of being left-handed, he held the instrument flat on his lap and played it much like a lap-steel. Since he was blind, he had no way of seeing how it was supposed to be held and, without a teacher, he learned it in his own way.

All this being said, left-handed guitars are much more difficult to find, much more expensive for what you get, and have substantially less selection than regular guitars. In the past, I have had students learn left-handed because they learned quite a bit on the instrument at home left-handed already and had their own left-handed guitar that they brought to school. An absolute beginner, however, should learn to play the instrument on a regular guitar.

Bass

Guitar and bass, although similar, have some very specific differences:

1. There are only four strings instead of six.
    a. They are tuned the same as the guitar but instead of E(6), A(5), D(4), G(3), B(2), E(1) it's just E(4), A(3), D(2), G(1). Its pitches sound an octave lower than the guitar.
2. They are typically played with the fingers instead of a pick.
    a. In heavier styles of rock music, the bass guitar can be played with a pick.
    b. The strings are not necessarily plucked, but instead *brushed* with the fingers.
3. The frets are wider than on a guitar.
4. The strings are longer and thicker than on a guitar.

For some learners, a full size bass guitar may be too big. Short scale bass guitars are designed for those smaller learners you may have. They are sized more like an electric guitar but are actually bass guitars.

This is a pickup but used as a thumb rest when playing bass guitar.

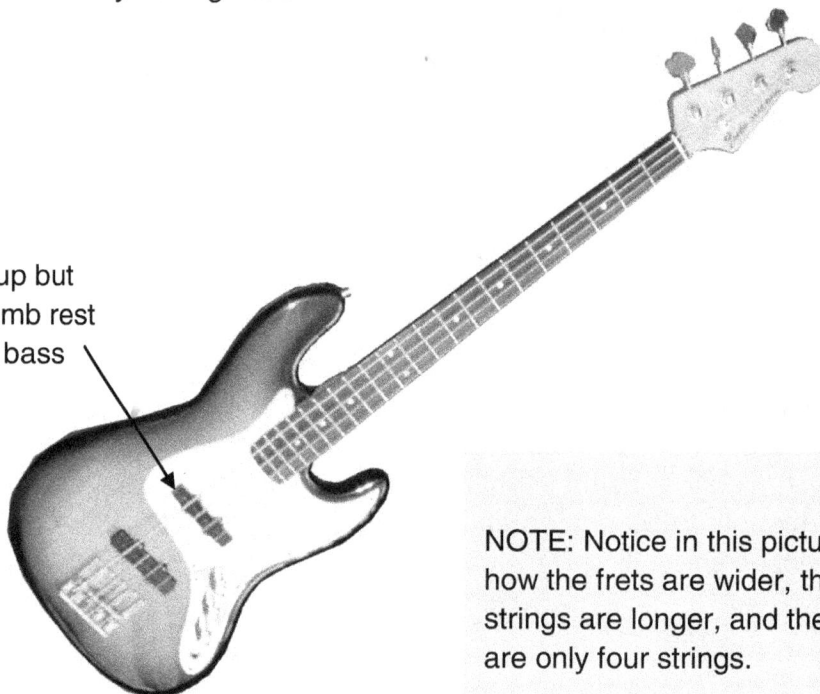

NOTE: Notice in this picture how the frets are wider, the strings are longer, and there are only four strings.

Bassists typically do not play chords, but instead the root notes of the chords. This means it is important for bass players to know how to "read" guitar chords and know where all of the notes are up to the first few frets at the very least. For example, they need to know that when a guitarist plays an Am chord, they play an open string A on the 3rd string or a 5th fret A on the 4th string (these are the same A).

Scale patterns for the instrument are the same but there are only four strings to work with instead of six.

Even though a bass player doesn't usually play chords, they should know what the chord tones are and where they are on the instrument. They don't always play the root—sometimes they play the 3rd or 5th depending on the song. This means that arpeggios are important as a bass player. Learning at least the minor, major, and dominant 7 arpeggio patterns are useful for writing songs or solos. Here are the basic arpeggio patterns for bass:

Major Arpeggio

Using the 4th finger on bass can be a challenge for many learners. It is common to use both the 3rd and 4th fingers together to give each more strength. They can be used separately as well. There are two schools of thought on this. Try it both ways:

Dashed line indicates an extension

5th Fret

This would usually be played using a finger roll. This means that it is played using the same finger but without lifting it for the next string. This is similar to a barre but instead of holding the strings down at the same time, you would simply change where the pressure is coming from the finger.

Minor Arpeggio

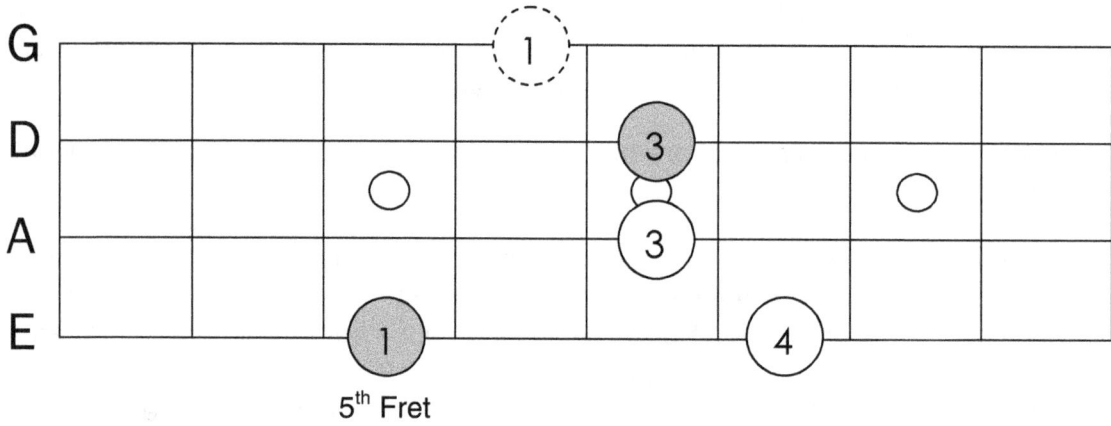

5th Fret

Dominant 7 Arpeggio

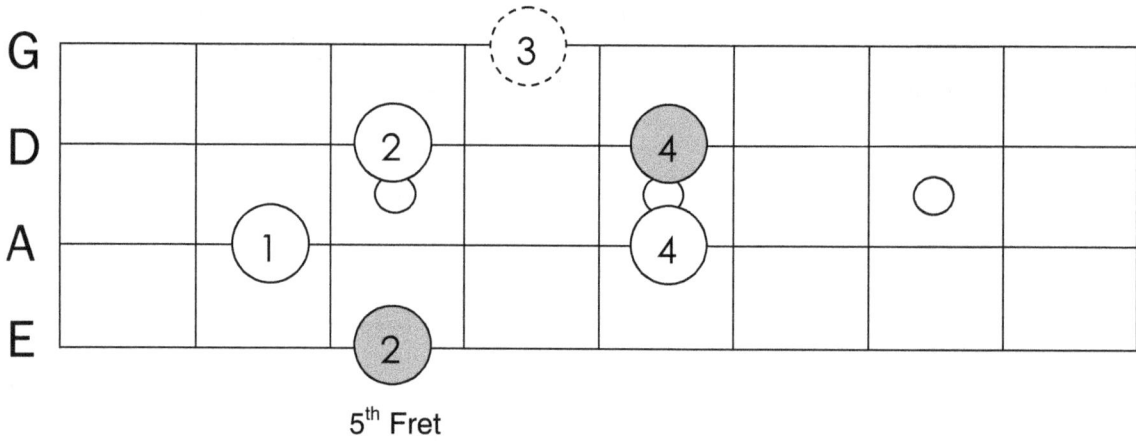

5th Fret

Drums

The drummers are the kings and queens of a band not only because they sit on thrones but because what they say, goes. By this, I mean that drummers usually dictate the style a band is playing in and set up the band for the next section of the song using fills. Many times, a great drummer can cover up weaker players in the group. They are the beat keepers. Something important to note however is that drummers, even though they are the beat keepers, do **not** play drum *beats*. They play *patterns* or *grooves.* This dichotomy is important because beats are what an audience feels while patterns and grooves are what an audience hears. Drummers play patterns and grooves **to** the beat.

Anatomy

Ride
Crash
Rack
Medium tom High tom
Hi-hats
Floor tom
Snare drum
Bass/kick
Micing hole

Holding the Sticks

Matched

Matched grip is the most common stick-holding technique in rock music. Each hand is holding the stick the same way. There are three main matched grips:

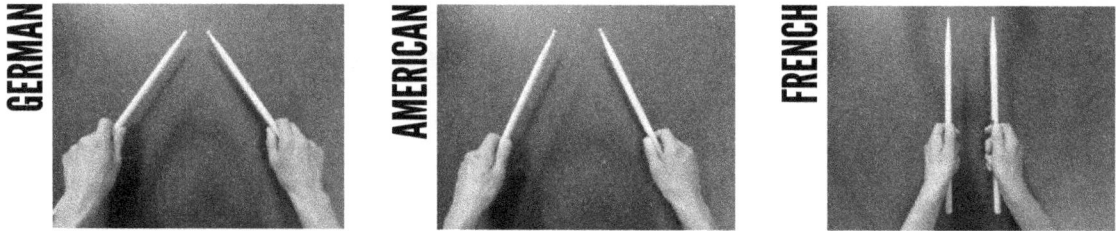

The French grip is most commonly used among timpanists in orchestras. It is characterized by the sticks being held in parallel with the thumbs up. All of these, however, will be used depending on what part of the drum kit you are playing at any given time and will vary naturally.

Traditional

Traditional grip is used in marching bands and sometimes referred to as the *jazz* grip. With this grip, each hand holds the stick in a different way. The right hand is a *regular* grip while the left hand grips the stick with the palm facing up. The stick sits between the thumb and two middle fingers. It was developed in the marching band idiom because the old leather straps holding up the snare drums in the marching band made the drum angle away from the player causing them to adjust their grip to compensate for the angle. With this, the traditional grip was born. There are a couple of common variations on this grip:

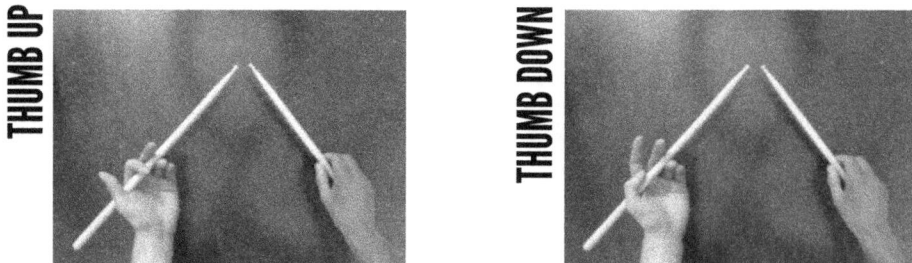

Whether you or your drummers choose matched or traditional is not important. The grip you choose should be comfortable and loose. Whatever they choose, there should be no pointed fingers. This is a common mistake for inexperienced drummers. This causes tension and does not let the stick bounce.

As a drummer myself, I find that sometimes the style will dictate the grip. If your drummers are fluent with multiple grips, encourage them to experiment with different grips for different styles.

Basic Drum Patterns and Grooves

Due to the repetitive nature of many drumming patterns in rock music, there are only two that are essential in learning and performing rock music successfully. There are variations on these patterns but they are not needed as long as the drummer can hit the crash on the down beat of a new phrase and perform a simple fill every four to eight measures without skipping a beat. 85% of rock tunes use one of these two grooves with slight variations on the bass drum, snare, or both. Others might be more complex but are, essentially, based on these two patterns. Give them a try!

Here are the two essential drum grooves used in rock music:

The Basic Rock Groove

Crash cymbal   Hi-hats

Bass drum   Snare drum

The Basic Blues Groove (AKA: The Power Ballad Groove)

The basic blues groove is a triplet based pattern in 4/4 time. The power ballad groove is exactly the same but I find it is better conceptualized in 12/8 because power ballads are typically slow. An example of a power ballad is "Never Tear Us Apart" by INXS.

Other Drum Grooves

There are a number of other drum grooves that drummers use depending on the style they are performing. Some of these grooves include jazz, reggae, samba, and bossa nova. However, these are very rarely or never used in rock music. The following two basic grooves are occasionally used in rock music:

Basic Disco Groove

Basic Shuffle Groove

Fills

Fills are what drummers play to set up the band for the next section of a song. For example, a drummer will usually play a fill going from the verse into the chorus so the band knows what is coming next. Fills are also used to indicate the end of a phrase and the beginning of a new one, which in rock music are usually every four or eight measures. Try playing these fills slowly at first using the sticking pattern provided and be sure to practice going right back in to the beginning of the phrase as indicated above.

BASIC FILL FOR A ROCK GROOVE

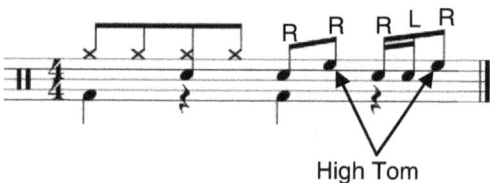

High Tom

BASIC FILL FOR A BLUES GROOVE

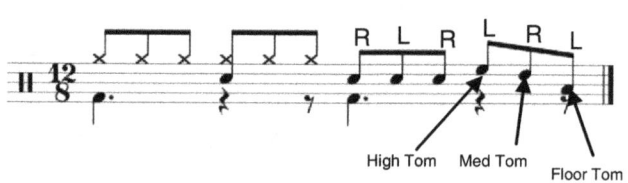

High Tom   Med Tom   Floor Tom

Drum Rudiments

Rudiments are like scales for drummers, they help with fluency and give you and your learners tools to use for solos and fills. There are five main rudiments on which all 40 are based. If you are only going to learn five rudiments, it should be these:

SINGLE STROKE ROLL

R L R L R L R L

DOUBLE STROKE ROLL

R R L L R R L L

SINGLE PARADIDDLE

R L R R L R L L

FLAM

L R   R L

DRAG

L L R   R R L

NOTE: All of these should be learned extremely slowly with proper sticking and consistent tone and gradually sped up and then slowed down again. Think of it as a pyramid.

Keyboard

Keyboards are, in many ways, a lead instrument in the rock band. It seems that the keyboard goes through phases of popularity in the history of rock music. For example, 80s bands are known for utilizing keyboards and keyboard synthesizers as lead instruments and as accompaniment instruments too. In recent times, electronic pianos have enjoyed a comeback in many modern rock ballads. Keyboards can add new sounds to tunes that have never been used, they can replace some instruments in situations where a particular instrument is not available and they can also reinforce harmonic structures in many rock tunes. However, before we continue, you should understand the difference between an electronic piano, a keyboard, and a synthesizer.

Electronic Piano

These are, in essence, pianos. They are usually bulky and difficult to transport and will have weighted keys and perhaps a few basic effects. If this is all you have, it will serve the purpose, it just won't have some of the iconic sounds of most 80s groups. An example of an electronic piano would be a **Clavinova**.

Keyboard

Keyboards usually serve as a hybrid between a piano and a synthesizer. They can range in size and often have keys that are thinner and not weighted. They include a large number of built in effects to cater to any style of rock music. Many have a pitch bend lever and ways to customize sounds. Keyboards are probably your best choice for this genre as they are very versatile.

Synthesizer

These are specialized keyboards that range in size from one octave to several octaves. They are designed to be completely customizable and each brand of synthesizer will have their own particular base sounds. **Moog** is a big brand of synthesizers that were extremely popular in the 70s and 80s with their own iconic sound.

Anatomy

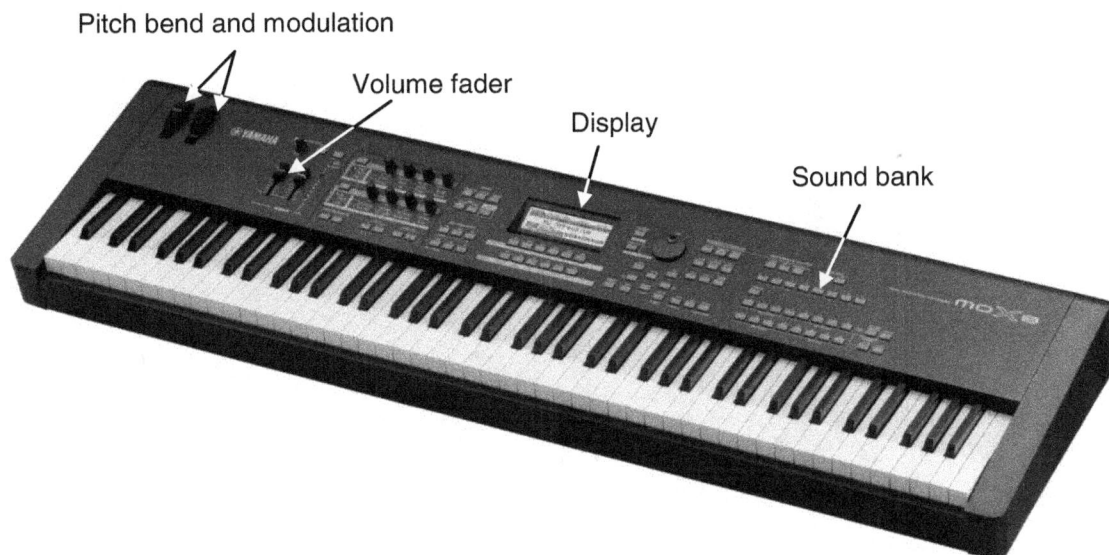

Pitch bend and modulation

Volume fader

Display

Sound bank

NOTE: Unlike guitar, bass, and drums, keyboards are all unique depending on the brand and model but most should be relatively similar to this one. Also, the back should have MIDI inputs and outputs, phones and line input and output as well as USB in and out, and DC power input. There is sometimes an input for a sustain pedal. Check your instruction manual for more in-depth descriptions.

Finger Numbers

Like in guitar, keyboard players have finger numbers as well except the thumb is counted:

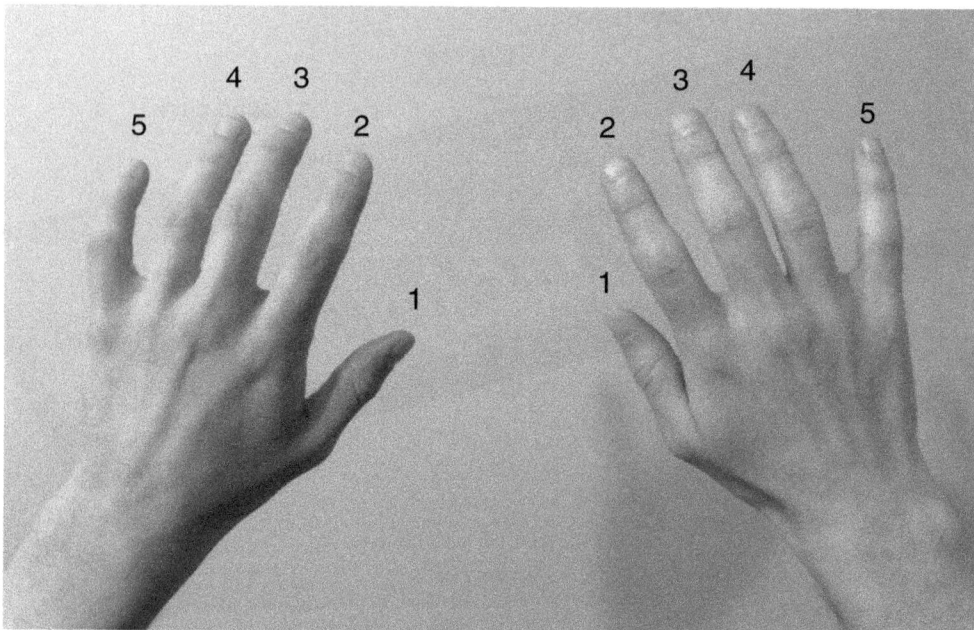

Chords

On the keyboard, chords are much simpler to form than on the guitar. There are no basic seven like in guitar because every chord has, more or less, the same hand form. Therefore, every chord is just as difficult as the next, meaning instead of chord *forms* or *shapes* like on the guitar, keyboard players need to be familiar with chord *formulas.* Even being able to hear the difference between major and minor is very helpful. The following are diagrams of the five types of chords they should know the *formulas* for. This means, they should know how to make them in any key. For the sake of simplicity, all chords will be shown for the right hand fingering and in the key of C. Take a look on the next page and experiment with these yourself:

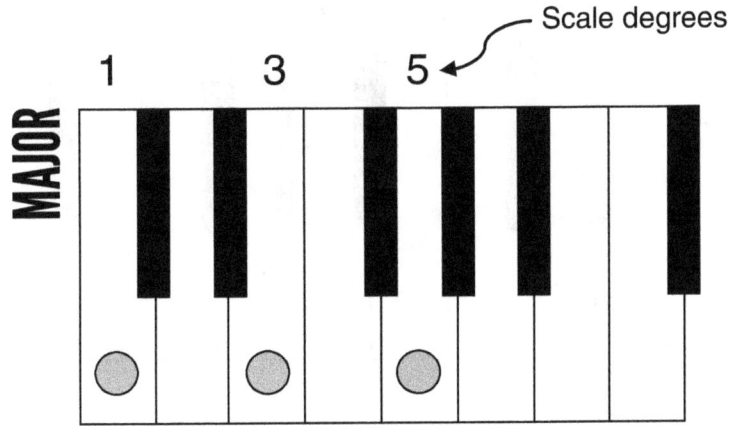

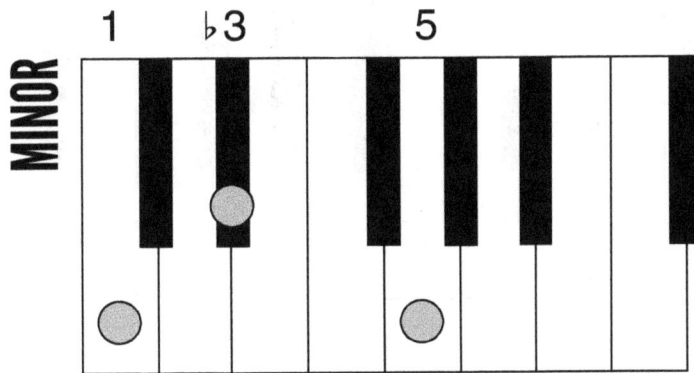

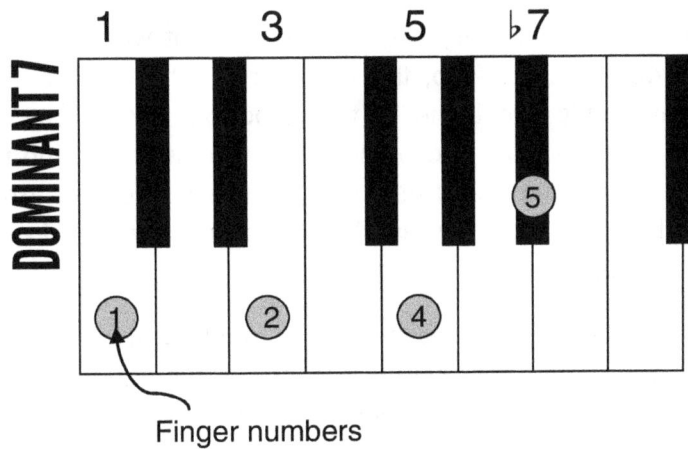

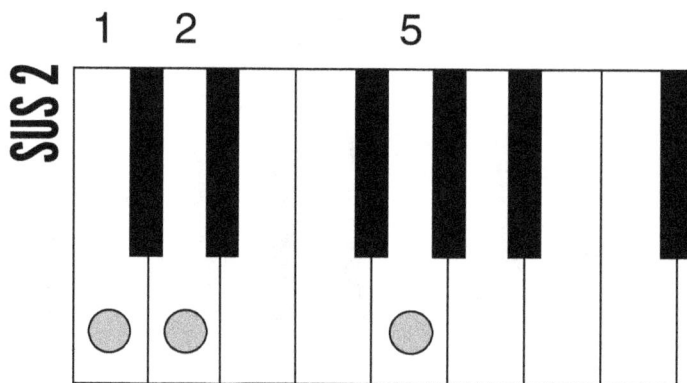

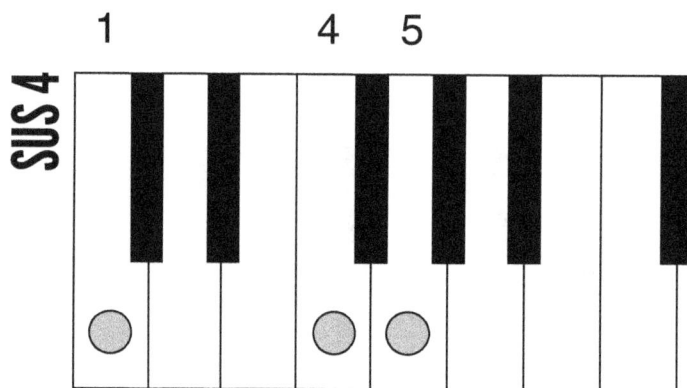

In all cases but the dominant 7 chord, the finger numbers are the same as the degree numbers for the right hand. However, depending on the key you are playing in, the fingering for other chords will vary slightly. Experiment with other keys to see what fingering is most comfortable. Also, the dominant 7 chord will be difficult for young learners with small hands. Move the ♭7 to the bottom, where possible, to make this easier. Using the thumb to play two piano keys at once is common in this genre. As well, learners could form the chord using two hands if need be. Another option is to take the ♭7 out all together leaving just the major chord for the keyboard and letting the guitar players cover the ♭7.

These chords are played with the right hand primarily, but what about the left hand? The left hand, in rock music, usually covers root notes instead of chords. Octaves are common but if octaves are not playable, fifths work great too. Sometimes, the left hand will be given its own line. An example of this would be "Don't Stop Believin'" by Journey. Following the bass line for the left hand is a great first step. Sometimes too, a song will not have any prominent keyboard parts. In this case I ask learners to follow the guitar part or ask them to make a part that works for the song.

Chord Chart

I have a *Piano Chords* chart on the wall close to my keyboard players that shows nine root position piano chords in every key. The types of chords it shows are: major, minor, diminished, augmented, dominant 7, minor 7, major 7, suspended 4, and major 6 for all keys. It is very useful for when there is a chord that your piano players don't know right away. They can quickly and efficiently look it up and keep on playing. As mentioned before, suspended 2 (sus2) chords are common but this chart does not include sus2 formations. Despite this, I find learners quickly pick up on this formula. This one can be found on Amazon.com but other posters like it can also be found elsewhere. A quick Google search will get you what you need.

Chord Inversions

Chord inversions are very common in rock music. I encourage my keyboard players to find the closest possible inversions after the root chord so their hands aren't moving all over the keyboard. If they can keep one or two of the pitches from the first chord and put them in the next chord, why move them? Many rock songs are already arranged in this manner. Use the chord voicings from the recording when possible and do not analyze the voicings with classical theory. Classical theory does not apply here, so you will notice a large number of second inversion chords. In a typical rock song, going from *I* to *IV* is extremely common, therefore playing the root position *I* chord to the second inversion *IV* chord is also common because it is the closest position to that chord.

Scales

Unlike guitar, keyboard players have to memorize every scale due to the fact that they do not have to memorize a single finger pattern. However, a good ear and a basic knowledge of the *scale formulas* can be very helpful. For example, if a learner doesn't know how to play an E major scale but knows that it starts on E and knows what it is supposed to sound like, they will be successful with learning and remembering the scale. Also if they don't know the scale but know the *formula*, they will also be successful. Below are four different types of scales they should become comfortable with. Again, for the sake of simplicity, the scales will be displayed in C.

If you know the major scale, all other forms of the scale come from that. The formula for the major scale is:

Whole Step (Tone) → Whole Step (Tone) → Half Step (Semi-tone) → Whole Step (Tone) → Whole Step (Tone) → Whole Step (Tone) → Half Step (Semi-tone)

Try them out:

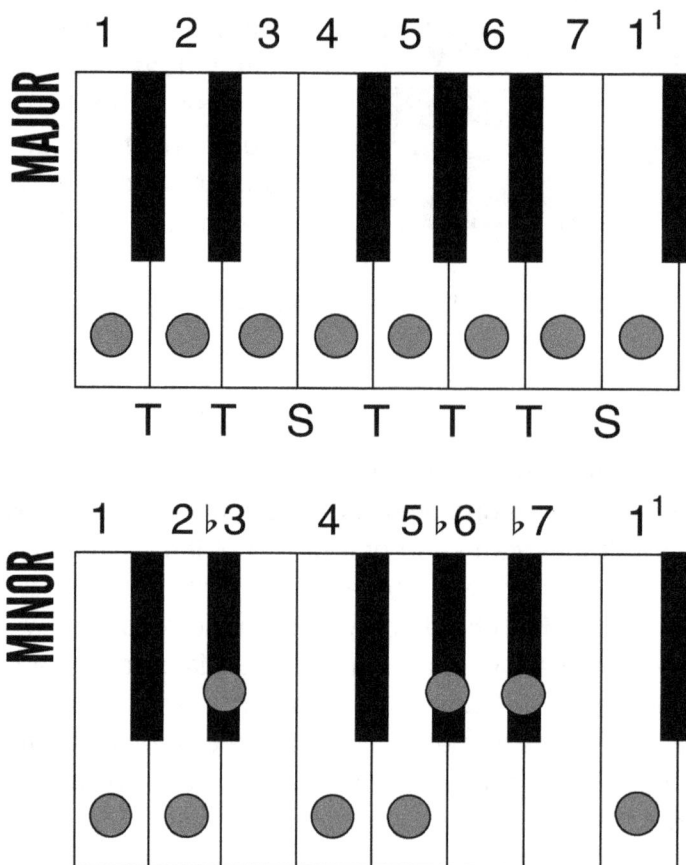

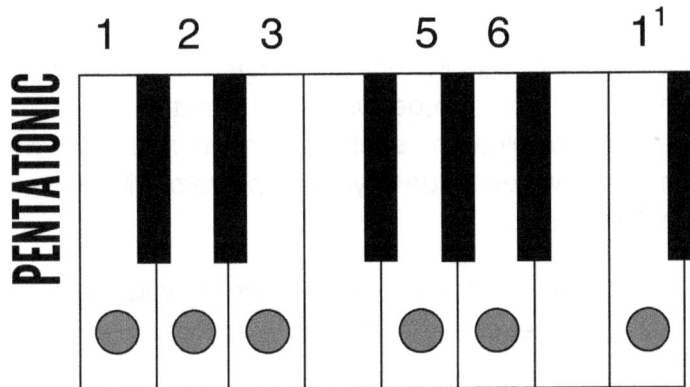

PENTATONIC

1   2   3   5   6 1^1

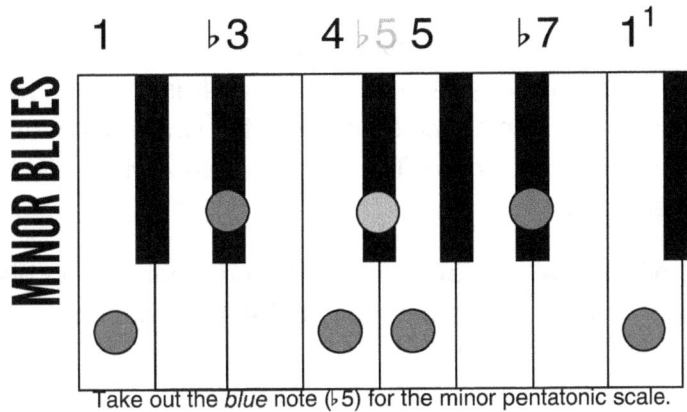

MINOR BLUES

1   ♭3   4♭5 5   ♭7 1^1

Take out the *blue* note (♭5) for the minor pentatonic scale.

The numbers above each pitch are derived from the major scale. This means that even if you don't know the intervals between each pitch in the scale (tone, semi-tone, etc.), you will be able to alter or skip particular scale degrees based on those numbers. For example, if you know a minor scale is just a major scale with lowered 3rd, 6th, and 7th scale degrees then all you really need to know is the major scale and which ones to skip or alter depending on your scale formula.

Effects

Effects are extremely important with keyboards. There are so many sounds that keyboards have to reproduce or create to perform a song authentically. Many keyboards have built in USB ports for downloading sounds from the internet or hooking up a laptop with a sound bank. However, your keyboard players will be successful with at least these five or similar sounds:

- *80s Brass:* Many forms of this effect are used in, you guessed it, a lot of 80s music. In particular, the song "Jump" by Van Halen as well as "The Final Countdown" by Europe.
- *Strings:* Used for backgrounds in a ton of ballads and slower tunes.
- *Fargo:* Another sound used in music from the 80s. This sound is similar to a phaser.
- *Grand Piano:* This one is pretty self explanatory.
- *Rock Organ:* Used in many blues-rock songs. It is characterized by a *Leslie Speaker* which is that iconic rock sound with the whirly speaker. Another name for this might be *Rhodes Organ.* The Deep Purple keyboardist uses this sound in many of their songs.

As mentioned, a **Clavinova** with a few different sounds that can be blended together will suffice—for now. However, the sounds will not be as authentic as they could be.

Vocals

Vocalists are, arguably, the most important musician in the rock ensemble. They command the most attention and audiences usually give it to them. It is also the one instrument that, with your eyes closed, will dictate the age of your group. What I mean is, a good elementary group will sound like a group of elementary students only when they sing. An older junior high or high school group would not necessarily give away their age through their singing voices. It is much less obvious because their voices are more mature. Because of this, it can be difficult to find music that fits the voices of your younger learners.

There are also many different ways to sing in a rock ensemble. Each vocalist in many classic groups has his or her own iconic sound that will indicate the group that is performing. For example, even if you are unfamiliar with a particular Aerosmith song, you will likely be able to recognize their sound by their vocalist, Steven Tyler. My general rule for learners is, do not try and sound like somebody else. Just try and sound like *you.*

Micing

Every brand of microphone is different but for best results, holding the microphone two finger widths apart from the mouth is a good rule of thumb. Or is it rule of *finger*? **Shure SM58**s are considered the industry standard in vocal microphones and have an incredibly clear sound but for a beginner might be difficult to use. What I mean by this is if the vocalist doesn't have the microphone pointing straight at their mouth and at least two finger's width from their mouth, it will be difficult to mix and may be completely inaudible. Other options for vocal microphones that are very high quality are the **Sennheiser e945** and the **Audio-Technica ATM29HE**. **The Audio-Technica ATM29HE** is actually a well designed instrument microphone that I have used as primarily vocal microphones for years. They have a wide pick-up radius and thus are extremely versatile. I have even used these as overhead choir microphones.

Basic Skills

Singers in a rock groups should have outstanding pitch retention and have good memorization skills. The section on auditions goes into pitch retention in more detail and how to choose the right singers for your groups.

Range

I have found that the tessitura for elementary singers is typically c^1–d^2. This being said, the older the singer, the lower and higher this can be extended. Some Grade 6 students that I have had were able to comfortably hit low g and get as high as g^2.

Bands that *generally* work really well for elementary voices that do not have to be transposed:

- Journey
- Europe
- Trooper
- Coldplay
- Hedley
- Avril Lavigne
- Foreigner

Chapter 8 discusses transposing and reasons why you might transpose music for your rock group—vocalists being one of those reasons.

Harsh Vocals

This refers to the extended vocal technique that is used on more aggressive styles of rock music such as punk and metal. Colloquially, we know it as screaming or growling. An individual that comes to mind that employs this technique is James Hetfield of the metal band, Metallica. Another lesser known individual is Corey Taylor of the Nü-Metal band Slipknot. Harsh vocals are used in many other styles of rock music as well to much lesser extremes. An example of this is Bryan Adams who uses harsh vocal sounds in many of his songs, especially in the higher registers. Although he definitely does not use this technique in the same way as James Hetfield or Corey Taylor, it is a form of harsh vocals that is stylistically appropriate. I realize that this is a hot topic for many classically trained vocalists but it is a legitimate vocal technique that can be taught to be delivered properly without destroying a person's vocal chords. This being said, even if I were trained in this style of singing, I would not teach it to young vocalists without a tried and proven method for doing so safely with young voices specifically. High school students have the vocal maturity to begin this training and may even begin inserting harsh vocals into their own music naturally. Sometimes this does occur because the music calls for it and many times they figure out their own way to do it that fits their voices without hurting their vocal chords. So, in some cases, just letting it happen can be your best bet. Every voice is different.

There are vocal coaches who are specialists in this area. Melissa Cross of *Zen of Screaming* is a classically trained vocalist who specializes in harsh vocals and has been hired by such bands as Coheed and Cambria, Machinehead, Disturbed, and many others. Corey Taylor, mentioned previously, has been a client of hers and is a vocal success story that can be traced back to his early Slipknot days. If you were to follow his career from the mid 90s to today, it is very clear he was destroying his vocal chords. At one point he changed his technique and began to change his sound drastically as he was learning the new technique with Melissa Cross. Hearing anything he does now, it is clear he has overcome his poor technique and is no longer hurting his voice.

> NOTE: I do not claim to be an expert in *Harsh Vocals* and this should not be taken as such. This section is simply to introduce you to a vocal styling you may not be familiar with and to give you a place to start if you want to find out more about this technique.

Horns

In this instance I don't mean French horn, I mean any wind instrument. Occasionally, there will be horn players in your groups. In certain styles of rock music like ska and funk, horns play a very prominent role. If the song you are learning has horns but your school has no horn players, synthesizers can reproduce the sounds of most horns without affecting the integrity of the music. In particular, the group INXS regularly uses a saxophonist but a saxophone setting on a keyboard/synthesizer works just fine. As well, some songs can have horns replace a keyboard/synthesizer if your group has real horn players. A lot of 80s tunes use the common synthesizer setting, *80s Brass*, for that iconic 80s synthesizer brass sound but why not use actual horns if you have them?

Micing

Micing a horn is just as important is micing a vocalist. A typical vocal or instrument microphone will, in most cases, do the trick. However, the best way to mic horns is to use clip-on microphones that clip onto the bell of each instrument. **AMT**'s line of wireless and belt-packless clip-on mics are very good quality and look very slick. Each one can be easily modified to fit any wind instrument. Many times, horn players and other musicians in rock bands need to move around, a clip-on microphone will allow the horn players to do just that. A stationary vocal or instrument microphone will not. I will be discussing stage presence and movement on stage in a later chapter.

Basic Skills

Typically, a horn player will know at least a B♭ major scale and arpeggio if they have been playing in concert band. However, its relative minor, G minor, or G Dorian (natural minor scale with a raised 6th scale degree) will be much more useful. Due to the prominence of guitars in rock music, sharp keys and blues patterns are very common. This means that becoming familiar with E, A, B, as well as G major and Mixolydian would be very useful for improvising. Blues and Dorian patterns in E, A, G, B, and C will also be quite useful to start. Learning these scales first, by rote and without notation, is not as difficult as it sounds because they are no longer *sharp* keys, they become scale patterns. As well, most horn parts will be learned by ear, so reading notation will not get in the way of learning the song and therefore sharps and flats become essentially irrelevant. Instead, patterns and pitches become fingerings or horn *tablature*. Tablature will be discussed in Chapter 6. Essentially, they will figure out ways to write it down or remember it without using traditional notation. Horn players will naturally discover alternate fingerings/slide positions for many pitches in the process. However, if your guitar players are relatively skilled at power and barre chords, you could have them easily transpose to a more horn-friendly key.

Brass Instruments

Brass instruments are unique because pitch range depends on the level and experience of the player. Therefore, learning a typical *Do* to *Do* scale may prove unsuccessful for a beginner. Here are a few ways to start with a beginner brass player in a rock band:

These would likely be best learned in combination with each other:

1. Learn the pitches in the B Mixolydian (lowered 7th) scale starting on E and descending to B, only ascending to high B after more playing, much like a B♭ major scale is learned. This is, essentially, a *Sol* to *Sol* scale but can be used in the keys of both E and B successfully.
2. Give them a root note and have them experiment with improvising this way.
3. Give them an easy horn line that only has three or four pitches to learn by ear. It could even be a vocal melody from one of the songs you are working on.

Remember, the first horn players in popular styles like jazz learned their instrument the same way rock musicians learn their instruments today. Famous jazz trumpeter, Louis Armstrong, sums this up nicely. After being asked if he could read music he is said to have replied, "Yes, but not enough to hurt my playing."[5] Therefore, it is important to not over-saturate your horn players with sheet music. They should learn to play the music by ear primarily much like other rock musicians. Refer to Chapter 6 for more on learning rock music authentically and the informal learning practices of rock musicians.

CHAPTER 5

Chapter 5: Repertoire

So you have your gear, your instruments, and the basics of how to play them. Now what? When I first began implementing my rock program, the most frustrating and time-consuming task was finding school appropriate songs that fit the skill level of the musicians in the band. This list is compiled from years of teaching rock bands at my school. This list also acts as a grading system, per se, for rock band music. Think of the concert band grading system as it relates to the skill level and experience of the musicians in the band but instead of B100 to B600, we have *Very Easy*, *Easy*, *Medium*, and *Difficult*. I am hoping that this list will provide you with a place to begin or a place to advance your rock bands at your school.

Song List

This list includes the song name, artist name, chords, and skills learned from each song. It is mostly catered to guitar players, but unless otherwise stated, you can assume that the keyboard, bass, drums, and vocals are pretty straightforward. This means that drums will play a straight-up rock groove variation, bass will play root notes more or less, and piano will play chords that basically follow the guitar, as well as easy vocal melodies. It is also important to note that the chords listed are not necessarily in order. They are simply a list of the chords in the song.

Using Chapter 4 as a guide and as you learn more about these instruments through experimenting on your own, knowing how to simplify many of these songs will become easier. Sometimes we don't perform the songs as on the recording. We may create our own arrangements by taking out a section to simplify it or there have been times where we have only performed what we know of a challenging *project* song. For me, it is about the process here—we rarely perform a song only once and if a song is only half learned, the next performance will be the entire song or an arrangement that works. This also creates lower stress levels for students and teachers. As well, if you recall, Chapter 4 covers easy versions of most basic guitar chords. Using these easy chords is one way to simplify many of these songs. It also discusses the relationship between barre chords and power chords. In many instances, power chords can replace barre chords without losing the integrity of the music.

Very Easy/Beginner

This level includes songs that have two or three, sometimes four chords only or a basic, repetitive riff for all instruments. They may also be primarily power chords but can be easily simplified by playing only the root notes. Drums will play a basic rock groove or blues variation or will work with a basic rock groove or basic blues groove. Sections of songs may be a little more of a challenge but, for the most part, are attainable or will still work with that section removed:

- **Never Tear Us Apart** by INXS (mostly keyboard: C/A, C^{sus4}/F, Dm, F, G) triplet feel, guitar is minimal. Chance for minor pentatonic or blues solo.
- **Best Day of My Life** by The American Authors (D, G) with easy guitar riff in the chorus. Beginning banjo riff can be omitted.
- **Should I Stay or Should I Go** by The Clash (D, G, A^7, G/F). Drums may find this difficult in chorus.

- **Stompa** by Serena Ryder (C, G, Am, Em, A^7, B^7 in bridge only). Easy riff based song in Em. Bridge is easy but may be difficult to remember because there is no obvious pattern. Bass drum part in the drums could be a challenge for a beginner drummer. However, a straight 4/4 rock groove is fine.
- **Blitzkrieg Bop** by The Ramones (power chords, *I–IV–V–I* progression). Could be quick for the drummers. Key of A.
- **Songbird** by Oasis (G, Em).
- **Good Riddance** by Green Day (G [with added 5th], C^{sus2}, D^{sus4}, $Em^{add \flat 7}$). The chord progression will make much more sense when you listen to it.
- **All Day and All of the Night** by The Kinks (power chords: F, G, B♭, A, C, D). Good one for improvising on G blues.
- **Lean on Me** by Bill Withers (C, F, G^7). Very easy for all instruments, can be a little low for singers. Easy root position chords in parallel motion for the keyboard. Riff based.
- **You Really Got Me** by The Kinks (power chords: F, G, A, C, D). This song presents a great opportunity to improvise in G minor pentatonic.
- **Eye of the Tiger** by Survivor (power chords: C, B♭, G, A♭, easy barring). Can be easily simplified, fits female voices nicely, keyboard has the following progression in the verse: Cm, A♭, B♭, Cm^{sus2} all in root position.
- **SONGS THAT ARE DIFFICULT BUT CAN BE EASILY SIMPLIFIED**
- **Sweet Home Alabama** by Lynyrd Skynyrd (D, C, G, one F chord). Without picking patterns or solos this is very easy to play.
- **Sweet Child o' Mine** by Guns n' Roses (D, C, G). No down-tuning, no solos and this song can be easily played.

Easy/Some Experience

This level includes basic chords, scales and concepts as well as some easy solos. Players who have had some lessons or experience, or are a quick learn and know the *Main 7* chords would be able to handle most of these songs. They may have started learning some power chords and barre chords but are still somewhat uncomfortable with them. Drums may have basic fills or an easy groove variation:

- **Enter Sandman** by Metallica (power chords). Can be done with first finger only and it still works. Some simple palm muting. Drumming can be complex at beginning but for the most part pretty straight forward. Remove whispered section of lyrics in the bridge.

- **Berlin Wall** by Town Heroes (capo 2, drop D tuning easy one-finger power chords). The drummers will love this one. A bit of a challenge in the bass drum but they love it once they get the hang of it.
- **If Today Was Your Last Day** by Nickelback (capo 1, easy barring, Bm, D, A, E, G)
- **Keep Holding On** by Avril Lavigne (G [with added 5th], G/F#, Em$^{add\flat7}$, C^{sus2}, Am, C, Em). This one will make more sense when you listen to it.
- **I Love Rock and Roll** by Joan Jett (power chords E, A, B, G. *I–IV–V–I* progression). Drums are really easy but there is a small turnaround in the chorus. Take out last verse lyrics and replace with first.
- **Proud Mary** by CCR (C, A, F, G, D, Bm). Strumming pattern might be a bit of a challenge at first.
- **Riptide** by Vance Joy (capo 1, Am, C, G, F). Solo before the bridge can be a bit of a challenge but the song will work well without it.
- **Christmas Love** by Billy Idol (G, C, D, A^7, D^7, Em, simple picking patterns).
- **Nothing Else Matters** by Metallica (Em, C, D, G, B, power chords, picking patterns) NOTE: I would begin without picking—just strumming.
- **One** by U2 (C, F, Am, G, easy one string picking).
- **Takin' Care of Business** by BTO (blues, power chords: C, B♭, F, F pentatonic/blues scales).
- **Takin' Care of Christmas** by BTO (power chords, blues).
- **House of the Rising Sun** by The Animals (Am, C, D, F, E^7, A minor pentatonic/blues scales) The progression can be a bit confusing.
- **Wish You Were Here** by Pink Floyd (G, Am, D, C, G, pentatonic scale).
- **What You Need** by INXS (F# easy/half barre, Am easy/half barre, B power chord, F# power chord). Great easy synthesizer solo. Easy guitar picking in bridge. Drum patterns change slightly in each section.
- **Island in the Sun** by Weezer (easy barring, Em, G, D, Am, C). Guitar players should be comfortable with the moveable four-string F chord shape.
- **Yellow** by Coldplay (capo 1, A, A^{sus4}, F#m, E, D, D^{sus2}, string bends).
- **Come Together** by The Beatles (B, A, and G power chords). Bass is a challenge throughout but repeats. The guitar solo can be turned into a keyboard solo and is very simple. Drums have a triplet fill at the beginning that comes up again near the middle of the song.
- **Boulevard of Broken Dreams** by Green Day (capo 1, Em, G, D, A, C, easy guitar solo). Make sure you change swear word to "messed" and use only an edited version. This is very easy to alter in any sound editing program. All you need to do is select the word and reverse it. Could be a bit low for some singers.

- **When I Come Around** by Green Day (power chords, F#, C#, D# [optional 5th string minor barre], B [optional 5th string major], *I–V–vi–IV*, G#, A#, B power chords). Make sure to take out the second verse and use the first verse twice. Also easy to alter on a sound editing program.
- **Astronaut** by Simple Plan (Dm, G, F, Am, C, basic strumming patterns).
- **Down on the Corner** by CCR (C, F, G). Lead guitar has an easy pentatonic melody throughout the song.
- **Free Falling** by Tom Petty (capo 1, E, A^{sus2}, B^{sus4}).

Medium/More Experience

This level includes basic chords as well as barre chords, picking patterns and some intermediate level solos. Basic drum grooves will work for the majority of these songs but will not work for a few of these if you want to keep the integrity of the song. There will be a mix of basic and more advanced keyboard parts.

This level encompasses a wide range of players and may include learners who are beginners or have some experience but are progressing quickly or need a good challenge. Use your discretion with this.

- **Happy Together** by The Turtles (capo 2, Em, C, D, G, B, fifth string major barre chords).
- **It's My Life** by Bon Jovi (power chords C, A♭, D♭, B♭, B, E♭, bridge has F, C, B♭). This can be played without the solo and still work.
- **Old Time Rock and Roll** by Bob Seger (basic blues pattern *I–IV* and *V* chords). Key of F#. Might be a bit of a hand stretch for your beginners. A great one to solo with F# minor pentatonic or blues.
- **Buddy Holly** by Weezer (power chords with lots of changes and jumps, down tuning by half step to play the bridge). I use Audacity to transpose this up by one half step instead of down-tuning the guitars. That way it is in the key of A.
- **Living on a Prayer** by Bon Jovi (C, D, Em, G). Off beat patterns, quarter note triplets, solo can be simplified, key change up a minor third but power chords will suffice. Keyboards are featured at the beginning and play an Em to G pattern in the verses.
- **Ghostbusters** by Ray Parker Jr. (A, E, B, power chords: B, A, G#, E). There are some awkward off beats in the guitar parts. What makes this the most difficult is the keyboard part. A good keyboard player should be able to handle it.

- **Kryptonite** by 3 Doors Down (Bm, G, A^{sus2}). Repetitive guitar picking pattern. A challenge for drummers.
- **Don't Stop Believin'** by Journey (power chords: B, E, C#, A). Drummers could find this song a challenge to keep steady, fits female voices quite nicely, bass line can be a challenge. Keyboard part can be done with right hand only as long as the bass part is strong. Have an additional keyboard player in charge of some of the other parts if your keyboard player can't reach the octaves.
- **Sweet Home Alabama** by Lynyrd Skynyrd: Without solos (D, C, G). Picking patterns, blues. Without picking patterns this song is much easier.
- **What About Love** by Heart (Dm, B♭, F, C). 5th string major barre chords, power chords, solo picking, a bit of scale work on the keyboard.
- **Let Her Go** by Passenger (Em, C, G, Bm, D). Changes are quick and the two progressions are similar enough to be a bit confusing.
- **21 Guns** by Green Day (Dm, B♭, F, C). 5th string major barre chords, power chords, solo picking.
- **The Final Countdown** by Europe: without solos (power chords: F#, D, B, E, F, A, G#). Palm muting, a good challenge for the keyboard player. Works without power chords but there are a lot of changes in the guitar part. Key of F#m.
- **The Boys in the Bright White Sports Car** by Trooper (all power chords: B♭, A♭, D♭, E♭). Some of the strumming patterns can be difficult for some guitar players. Intermediate to advanced guitarists could play the solos in this song. They are based mostly on the blues and minor pentatonic box patterns. Could be a great opportunity for improvised solos too.
- **Times like These** by Foo Fighters (Am, C, Em, D as well as E, D and C power chords). Intermediate solo picking. The big challenge in this song is the drums and the metre changes. There are many places where the time switches to 7/4 and then to 8/4 and back again. You need strong drummers for this tune.
- **Separate Ways** by Journey (power chords: E, D, C, B). Palm muting, easy harmonics. Keyboards have Em, D, C and a bit of easy solo riff work at the beginning middle and end. Drummers have a couple solos, a good chance for them to improvise.
- **I Wanna Rock** by Twisted Sister (power chords, A, G, D, E). Strumming pattern could be a challenge for limited knowledge player. Some intermediate level drum fills.
- **Summer of '69** by Bryan Adams (D and A power chords as well as A, D, G, F, B♭, C, and Bm). 5th string major and minor barre chords. Switches are pretty quick at times.

- **Clocks** by Coldplay (capo 1, D, Em, Am, G, F). 8/8 grouped as 3+3+2, keyboards have some advanced arpeggiation with E♭, B♭m, Fm, dual keyboard. Drummers will be challenged to keep steady and follow the 3+3+2 pattern.
- **Juke Box Hero** by Foreigner (power chords, D, E, B, G). Bridge can be a bit of a challenge. Vocals can be quite a challenge to pull off properly. Some more advanced drumming in areas (ie: switching feel).
- **Jump** by Van Halen. Guitars follow the bass line throughout this song. This is a keyboard feature and may present a challenge for a beginner keyboardist. Some of the drumming is quite advanced in places. Charts for this are easy to find. We performed this without the extended solo sections for guitar and keyboard.

Difficult/Lots of Experience

This section includes all basic chords and/or all barre chord forms as well as medium to advanced arpeggiation, medium to advanced solos and some advanced picking and finger pick-ing patterns or metres. This level will be a good challenge for any groups within your higher-end *Medium* category:

- **Fix You** by Coldplay (capo 2, C, C/B, Am, F, G). Guitar part is fairly minimal and simple. What makes this one difficult are the keyboard parts, some of the drumming and the vocal harmonies at the end. This will be easier with two keyboard players.
- **Sweet Child o' Mine** by Guns n' Roses (down tuning, D, C, G). Intermediate to advanced arpeggiation, picking patterns, power chords, bends, solo picking, some advanced bass lines.
- **Christmas All Over Again** by Tom Petty (A ,F#m, Bm, E, Gm, barre chords).
- **Take on Me** by A-Ha (Bm, E, A, D, A/C#, F#m, G). 6th and 5th string barre chords. A challenge for your singers and keyboard players.
- **Stairway to Heaven** by Led Zeppelin (finger picking, Am, C, G, D, FM^7). Barreing, challenging for all instruments and voices.
- **Dream On** by Aerosmith (finger picking, bends, some advanced solo picking).
- **Blackbird** by The Beatles (finger picking). In G.
- **Oh! Darling** by The Beatles (E+, A, E, F#m, A^7, D, F^7, Bm^7, B♭^{7}). 5th and 6th string major, minor, major 7 and minor 7 barre forms, blues and triplet feel for drums and keyboard, arpeggiation, picking patterns, a challenge for your guitar players. The bass line is quite a challenge as well.

- **Barracuda** by Heart (power chords). Palm muting, simple to complex metre changes. 4/4 to 5/4 and 4/4 to 3/4. Drums and guitars have the biggest challenge with all the metre changes and some of the drumming is quite advanced in places.

CHAPTER 6

Chapter 6: Learning and Performing Rock Music Authentically

It is important, when learning and teaching rock music, that it is learned in a culturally appropriate and *authentic* manner. This means that it should be learned in the way that it has traditionally been learned; through imitation, by rote, and by ear. Specifically, it should **not** be learned and understood using the conservatory method of music learning. No person can play rock music authentically using concert band instruments with written sheet music and a conductor in front of them. This chapter explores my own experiences and observations as well as research from around the world on the topic of *informal learning* with a specific focus on the way popular musicians learn.

Informal Learning

Informal learning is described as, essentially, learning methods that are used outside of a formal school setting and usually involves:

- Self-teaching.
- Copying recorded music.
- Regular composing, improvising, and listening practice throughout the learning process.
- Learning new skills based on interest rather than using a particular method.

Basically, it is how music has been transmitted and learned since it was first made by the first cavemen around a fire since the beginning of time. Something else that is important to note is that relying on standard notation is not expected and not needed to be successful in the rock and popular music scenes. Standard notation was only developed due to the lack of audio recording equipment before the 1900s. Some forms of notation have become standard in the popular music world like *tablature* and the *Nashville Number System*. These will be described and discussed later in this chapter.

Besides what was mentioned at the beginning of the book, there are a number of specific skills that musicians in this genre require and learn through informal means. There are kids in your schools that have an incredibly high skill level and know more than they can say—but can definitely play. This is especially true at the late intermediate and high school levels but is possible at any level of school instruction. Chances are they know or will know many or all of these skills and concepts without the guidance of a teacher. Many of my friends and fellow musicians who have primarily learned their craft informally can demonstrate the following:

> 1) **The ability to learn a song quickly, just from listening to it.** This skill also includes the ability to play in any key, knowledge and recognition of common chord progressions or patterns such as 12-bar blues.
>
> 2) **Knowledge of what fits in and around the beat** even if they are not able to put it into words. This is often referred to as feel and sometimes called fitting into the *groove*.
>
> 3) **Knowledge of roles of instruments in particular styles.** For example, the function of a bass and drums part in reggae would be much different than the interplay between bass and drums in heavy metal.

4) ***The ability to reproduce any sound effect as close as possible*** and use live and recording sound equipment.

5) ***The ability to read different forms of notation such as tablature, chord charts, and occasionally standard notation.*** It is important to note that notation plays a very different role in informal learning. It is used more as supplemental material or a way to help the performer remember a part. It is not a major learning resource as in traditional conservatory music education.

6) ***The ability to improvise and compose in any key with fluency.*** Improvising, composing, and copying are practiced throughout the learning process and are not compartmentalized into separate specialties. They become the true sense of being a musician—a performer, composer, improviser, and imitator.[6]

NOTE: The skills listed above were compiled from a combination of my own experience and Lucy Green's book, *How Popular Musicians Learn: A Way Forward for Music Education.*[6]

Listening

Listening is a fundamental skill in all types of music but when learning rock music it is emphasized due to the fact that music, in this genre, is transmitted primarily through audio recordings. There are two kinds of listening that informal learners engage with to learn a song that are worth considering when learning a new song with your groups:

1) **Active Listening:** This is when a group listens to a song with the active goal of learning it. Forms of active listening include *ghosting* (playing along without making a sound), listening for a specific instrument, trying to learn a part or any listening involved in actively learning a song.

2) **Passive Listening**: This is the homework that I primarily assign to my groups. I ask them to listen to a song a number of times or have it on repeat on their phones or at the very least, include the song in their playlists. They

learn the song the same way any person can memorize the lyrics of their favourite tunes without actively learning them.

Both of these ways of listening are mentioned in Lucy Green's work as well.

During my undergraduate degree, the focus was on notation and theory. It got in the way of me actually learning to improvise and compose. It was only after my music degree that I learned to improvise on the trombone *because I was free to experiment*. By-ear-learning and *good ears* develop much quicker in rock musicians due to their constant listening, copying, and improvising. Their ears do not necessarily develop to be any better than a classically trained musician but they definitely get better sooner. My ear has developed much faster in the last 10 years teaching music with guitar than it has in all of the years of prior musical training. This is likely due to the fact that I was and still am constantly copying and learning parts from recordings to help coach learners through their songs. In university, we had an ear training course that was separate and seemingly unrelated to the rest of our degree or instrument. There were few opportunities for *practical* uses of these aural skills due to the reliance on sheet music.

By-Ear-Learning

As mentioned in a previous chapter, when asked whether he could read music, jazz great Louis Armstrong is said to have replied, "Yes, but not enough to hurt my playing."[7] Learning by ear is a skill learned through doing it in context and informal learning presents multiple opportunities for this contextual learning. Informal musicians rarely have to sight-read to learn a song. This is an important part of teaching rock music authentically. Although playing by ear and reading music are often separated, playing by ear may be the most foundational of musical skills. It helps everything else. Think about it: playing by ear is like being able to copy a language just by hearing it. If you don't know the language, or can't remember or recognize enough of it, most people wouldn't even be able to copy back vows for their wedding. Much like learning a language, a pre-existing, ear-based fluency helps a musician understand written notation more easily. You never teach a baby to read before it learns to speak. How does a baby learn to speak, you ask? By copying, and experimenting. Once they understand the language and can speak it, they learn to read it and understand its notation. In a later chapter, I will take you through the process that I use that stays true to the informal learning practices of rock musicians that helps learners to focus on *by-ear-learning*. It is the essence of *sound before symbol*.

From my own experience in bands working with other popular musicians and my own by-ear-learning experiences, musicians with more by-ear-learning practice tend to employ these four strategies when learning a new song:

1) Listen for specific instrument sounds, recognizable timbres, or idiomatics: An example of this would be recognizing an open bass string or a guitar chord based on the voicing of the strings. An open D chord will always have the third on the top and has a very distinctive sound. A very common and instantly re-cognizable extension on guitar is going from a D to D^{sus4} and back again. One particular song that jumps out as containing this extension is in the opening of Bon Jovi's "Dead or Alive." As well, many rock musicians can re-cognize a blues pattern right away which develops with years of by-ear-learning, drastically cutting down the learning time.

2) Listen for the bass part: Musicians often listen to the bass part and try to learn the patterns being played. From there, they try chords based on those pitches. This is where I started when learning new songs. I suggest you begin with this too, if you are new to the process.

3) Listen for the melody: This involves using bits of the melody to figure out what chords are next. For example, if a melody changes chords on the second scale degree, a musician might use a dominant chord to see if it fits.

4) Listen for chord tones: If there is a particular chord tone that is jumping out to you, find it and form a chord around it. I have used this strategy myself and it can be very effective for some more obscure voicings.

For more on this, take a look at an article written by KG Johansson called "What Chord was That? A Study of Strategies Among Ear Players in Rock Music."[8] Some of these ways of learning by ear are mentioned in Johansson's article. There is also a 2010 study by Dr. Lucy Green discussing the ways in which students approach learning by ear called "Musical 'Learning Styles' and 'Learning Strategies' in the Instrumental Lesson: Some Emergent Findings from a Pilot Study."[9]

Inspiration from the Legends

Consider these quotes from some of the most famous and successful musicians in the world:

All of these quotes come from an article written by Lars Lilliestam called "On Playing By Ear."[10]

After being asked 'how do you formalate a song?,' Eric Clapton replied....

"You don't really, you just play around on the guitar and it formulates itself."

Eric Clapton, Yardbirds

"...we hardly have to say anything and then we do what [each other] means. We have a unique language together ... we have shaped our own expressions and our own rules that we follow."

Helena Nygren, Goteburg

"I very rarely think of what chords or what notes or where I put my finger...I don't think musicians who can really play think of music like that...to make it your own requires street learning. You cannot learn that in Harvard or Berkeley—that you have to learn from the streets, and that's my approach to music. The street university is very important, man."

Carlos Santana, Santana

"The good thing about the guitar was that they didn't teach it in school. Teaching myself was the first and most important part of my education. I know that Jeff Beck and I enjoyed pure [classical] music because we didn't have to. I hope they keep it [guitar] out of the schools."

Jimmy Page, Led Zeppelin

Perhaps keeping true to the informal ways in which these musicians learn would change Jimmy Page's mind.

Performing the Same Song Multiple Times

In the real world of performing, no professional ensemble or rock group performs a song once and then never plays it again. Why do we constantly do this in school? It is not an authentic representation of what it is like to be a performer. Rock bands, in particular, perform the same song multiple times. The first performance of a song is not usually the best performance because it's a process. Bands have to *road test* songs before they become a mainstay in their sets. This means that the song has to sit well with the band and with the audience. My learners never perform a song just once in the year. They get better and better at it each time over multiple opportunities to perform. This process focus helps learners to realize that it doesn't have to be absolutely perfect each time and they will always have a second and sometimes third or fourth chance to perform the song again. Not only is *feel* more important than the ability to read notes, it is also more important than *right notes* in a sense that an occasional wrong note will not be heard by the band and that a wrong note does not carry the same stigma it does with classical music. It is generally much more casual. It cuts down on stage fright and stress on the part of the facilitator and the learners. Think about how many times in your performing life that you performed a piece more than once. You could probably count how many times this happened on one hand.

How do I Teach it to Them and Where Do I Find the Charts?

As mentioned previously, many rock musicians learn primarily by rote or by ear but there are at least two very commonly used notational systems widely used by rock musicians. However, the notation used in this genre is not used in the same way that we typically use notation in a classical setting. The two main notational systems are *tablature* and the *Nashville Number System*. *Tablature* is primarily used for imitation and song transmission, and is typically found online, and in "How to Play..." books and other such literature. The *Nashville Number System* is used for both learning how to play and composition but also in performance using a system of vocal cues related to the notation. Here is an explanation of both systems:

Tablature

Tablature, usually shortened to *tab*, is a very common way of notating music for any fretted instrument such as a guitar, banjo, or ukulele. Guitar tablature, as it is today, evolved from the tablature of lute transcriptions from the Middle Ages.[11] [12] Informal ways of playing and performing music were common in the Middle Ages as they are today. Without recorded music, it only made sense to find ways to write these songs down and tablature was a very practical way to do so.

Tablature can be adapted for any fretted string instrument. Guitar, having six strings, has a six-line staff. Numbers signify what frets to press down and on what string. *Figure 1* (next page) shows a C major scale written in Western notation and the same written directly underneath it in tablature. Because tablature does not indicate rhythm, many times tablature published in books will have some kind of traditional notation accompanying it to indicate rhythm as in *Figure 1*. However, much of the tablature on the internet has no notated rhythm because the person who *tabbed it out* assumes that the person learning it already knows how the song goes. The reason the song is learned in the first place is because that person likes the song. That person learns it by ear, and instead of showing it to a real-life person, posts his or her transcription on the internet for all to enjoy. The next person hears that same song and searches for tablature on the internet and the cycle continues much like it would in a face to face situation. Also, the fact that much of the online tablature is learned by ear by

NOTE: To help with your understanding of this form of notation, think of any song and see if you can find it online! Type the song name with the word "tabs" beside it.

amateurs makes it inaccurate many times but there are always people logging on to update tablature so that they become more accurate with time. This is also why it is important to trust your own ears and to use tablature simply as a way to guide you or your learners in the right direction.

FIGURE 1

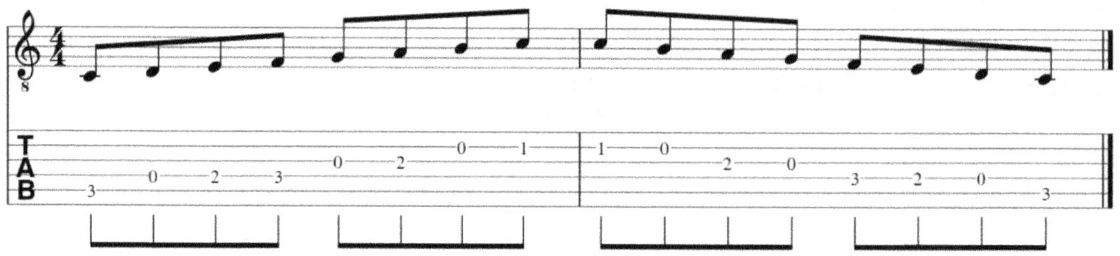

Tablature uses a six-line staff for guitar where each line represents a string on the instrument. Bass guitar has four lines. The bottom line is the thickest, lowest sounding string. The numbers represent the fret number to be played on that string. Stacks of numbers imply harmony and separated numbers imply melody much like standard notation.

Using a composition of mine I will show three different, but common, ways you might see tablature written:

Notes and Rhythms are Notated Above the Tablature

If you understand standard music notation this one is pretty straight forward. The top staff is the actual written pitches and the bottom line is the exact same part written in tablature. This is the form most commonly seen in published books.

TABLATURE EXAMPLE

Steve Giddings

Rhythms are Notated With the Tablature

In this example, the rhythms are written underneath the fret numbers and attached to them. Eighth notes, quarter notes, and sixteenth notes are recognizable almost instantly. Half notes are more difficult to differentiate. Since there are no note heads, the stem is slightly altered by simply making the stem shorter:

TABLATURE EXAMPLE (NO STAFF)

Steve Giddings

Half note

No Rhythms or Pitches—Just Tabs

You have to know how the song goes to play this. In most cases, people looking up tabs in this manner already know how the song goes. It's the reason they looked it up in the first place—it's a favourite of theirs. This is the most common type of tablature you will see on the internet usually *tabbed out* by amateurs on sites like *UltimateGuitar.com*. Occasionally there will be some attempts made to indicate rhythm and metre but for the most part, there are none. Due to it being *tabbed* by amateurs, it is not always accurate but does get better over time because others update the tabs on these sites. Many tabs like this will include their own legend for symbols they might add. Here is what the previous examples look like in this type of tablature:

TABLATURE EXAMPLE (INTERNET)

Tablature also has other types of notational symbols much like traditional notation to indicate various elements such as pitch bending and slides. Here is a list of symbols you might come across on a site like *UltimateGuitar.com*:

H: Hammer-on
P: Pull-off
B: Bend string up
R: Release bend
/: Slide up
\ : Slide down
V: Vibrato
T: Tap
X: Heavy damping

Here are a few examples of what you might come across with tabs written in published books. Go ahead and try some:

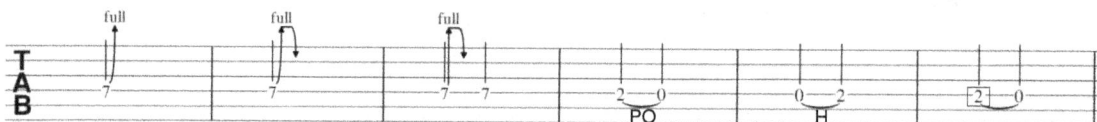

String Bend	Bend/Release	Prebend/Release	Pull-off	Hammer-on	Tap
This example shows bending the string so it sounds a full step higher, there are also ½ bends and ¼ bends.	This example shows bending the string so it sounds a full step higher, then bending it back down.	This is when the string is bent before it is plucked and then back once it is plucked.	This is done in the left hand only and happens when the player releases their finger and plucks the string at the same time.	This is the opposite of the pull-off but done in combination with the right hand. The player plucks the first pitch of the slur with the right hand and plays the second one without picking by using the left hand.	Taps are like hammer-ons but are performed with the right hand and are usually played in partnership with hammer-ons.

The Nashville Number System

The country music scene in Nashville is unique for its use of notational systems and musical language that has developed within Nashville and has become widespread throughout the continent as a legitimate form of musical notation. This notation is called the *Nashville Number System*, a versatile, short-hand, informal form of music notation.

Developed by Nashville country musicians, the Nashville Number System is used in every performance situation and facilitates easy transposition employing a combination of Western notation and numbers. This system uses numbers to indicate a chord within a specified key. For example, if you or your students were playing in the key of C and saw a "5" on the chart, they would play a G chord for that measure. The numbers in this notation refer to scale degrees rather than fret numbers. Western notation written above the numbers, indicates a melody. This chart, hand written for authenticity, explains how the Nashville Number System works on a basic level:

This is one measure.

This is an eight-measure phrase

Nashville Number System

1   2⁻   4 5   1

6⁻   4   1 5   1

This underline indicates that there are two chords in this measure. Each would be played for two beats.

Translates to:

These are the chords in the key of C.

C   Dm   F G   C

Am   F   C G   C

NOTE: There are a number of other symbols that notate various other musical elements and for a more detailed explanation and walk through on this system, look up Chas Williams. He has a book called *The Nashville Number System* and has a couple of very good videos explaining many of the possibilities of this notational system.

The Nashville Language

Any formally trained musician knows what the guitar player means when they say "a shuffle in Charlie with a fifty-five eleven turnaround," right? This colourful language is used by musicians throughout the country and blues scenes in the United States. Mayne Smith, author of an article titled "A Shuffle in Charlie: Technical Comm-unications Among Improvising Musicians," discusses many of the ways in which these musicians communicate within a performance setting. One extremely common way that many musicians communicate is by "reading" guitar chords,[13] meaning they follow along with the other players by watching the hands and fingers of the other guitar player. I've done this plenty of times while jamming tunes I don't know and it is very effective. Other ways include simple body movements and musical elements that indicate a chord change. It might be something as simple as a moving the neck of the guitar up and then down to indicate a change.

"A shuffle in Charlie with a fifty-five eleven turnaround" can be translated into terms that formally trained musicians in North America will understand: "Play a shuffle in the key of C starting with a G chord for two measures and then a C chord for two mea-sures." The fifty-five eleven refers to the Nashville Number System, which would be notated as 5 5 1 1 (G G C C). I have not used the Nashville Number System with my learners yet but it is a great way to notate new compositions or remember a particular pattern. A high school rock group *should* understand this system if they expect to perform rock and country music after graduation. It really helps them to understand theory in a very practical way and helps them to write down their compositions in timely fashion for later reference if they need to. Even if they don't use it later on, this is a very effective tool for learning music theory because it forces students to learn their key signatures and understand which chords belong to a particular key.

Resources for Learning Rock Tunes

- **GuitarJamz by martyzsongs on YouTube**
  - This channel contains a collection of guitar lessons that are very well paced and extremely accurate. It is my go-to place for learning guitar parts. I also refer a lot of my more independent learners to martyzsongs.

- **Songsterr**
  - This app is a collection of tabs for pretty much any song in existence for all instruments. The drum tab on Songsterr is pretty straightforward to understand. It uses the six line staff with rhythm but instead of numbers to indicate frets, it uses letters like 'S' for snare and 'BD' for bass drum. The tabs can sometimes be slightly inaccurate but it is a great resource to help get started or to figure out a tricky portion of a song. I use it mostly for figuring out guitar solos.
- **UltimateGuitar.com and AZLyrics.com**
  - UltimateGuitar.com has tabs, lyrics, and chords to help you through learning a song. They are not always accurate but pretty close a lot of the time.
  - A–Z Lyrics is a website that I have found to be the most accurate when it comes to making lyric books for your singers.
- **Your ear**
  - It is amazing how valuable our ears actually are as trustworthy re-sources. It took me some time to develop the ear that I have now. With practice, anything can get better. If you recall, earlier in this chapter, I discuss research behind learning by ear and how rock musicians learn songs by ear.
- **Band in a Box**
  - This piece of software for Windows is designed for improvising. You input the chord progression and everyone can solo over it.
- **Fake books and Real Books**
  - Fake books are very common with jazz musicians. They began as thick books with handwritten melodies and chords for hundreds of jazz stan-dards written out by jazz musicians and circulated within jazz circles. They come in B♭, E♭, and C versions for jazz musicians. These books contain enough information for the musicians to *fake it*, hence the name.
  - Real books are the published versions of these books and have ex-panded to include many more genres of music, including rock.
- **iReal Book Pro**
  - This app is directly based on the Real Book series of books. It works similarly to *Band in a Box* but is much easier to use and you can input your own chords or download progressions from the Real Books to find songs to practice improvising. You can edit almost everything about the progressions, from chord types to tempo and even key.

- **Steve's Music Room (www.stevesmusicroom.com)**
  - o My website contains information that can help you get your band off the ground. The blog is updated regularly with information on teaching rock bands but also a number of other music education topics.
- **Musical Futures (www.musicalfutures.org)**
  - o This website is based on Lucy Green's work on how popular musicians learn. Musical Futures is a program being implemented in many UK schools and some schools in Canada. Once you figure out how to navigate the site, there are a plethora of resources for coaching rock bands.

CHAPTER 7

Chapter 7: Auditions

The extracurricular bands at my school are auditioned groups. As much as I would love to take everyone in the rock band, I can't. I usually have between 50 and 80 auditions in any given year. Auditions can be as formal or as informal as you like. This chapter will give you an overview of how I run my auditions, present ideas about how auditions can look, and what I believe about auditioning.

Introduction to Auditions

Auditions take time and focus. At my school, auditions for the band is the most popular extracurricular activity. September and October every year are devoted to band auditions. Even if you think that you know your learners well, this step is still vital. At best, there will be a student that surprises you or really comes out of their shell. At worst, your learners will be provided with valuable audition experience that they will be able to use throughout their lives. In the end, auditions are worth the time invested into them. When I first began auditioning students for the band, I required them to have some lessons on the instrument. I soon realized that, in the spirit of true *informal learning* (see Chapter 6), students can and will play extremely well without private lessons and typically do this more often than not.

At the elementary level, at least, about one third of the auditions are for drums while another third of the auditions are for singing and the last third are for guitar, piano, and bass combined. Imitation is big. If a beginner can imitate with little guidance, they will be successful. I always have charts to help me remember what each student did.

Here is an overview of how auditions for the band work. For each instrument I have given the time required for the audition, minimum required skills, ideal skills, and the audition chart used for it with an explanation on how the chart can be used. Keep in mind that these are suggestions for auditions. You may find a method that works best for you. These are just what have worked best for me and if you are at a loss, are a great place to start.

Minimum Required Skills are skills needed to be successful in the rock band. If they possess these basic skills, they will be successful in reproducing the music as closely as possible:

Guitar

Required Audition Song: none.

Time Required: 7–10 minutes.

Minimum Required Skills:

> **Chords:** C, G, D, Em and ability to imitate power chords or barre chords or form them with guidance. Easy versions of chords are acceptable.

Scales: ability to imitate a basic *Minor Pentatonic Box Pattern* (see Chapter 4) as closely as possible.

Ideal Skills:

Chords: the *Main 7* (see Chapter 4) plus F, power chords, and barre chords.

Scales: minor pentatonic, blues, major, minor.

Lots of experience playing by ear and the ability to read some tablature and chord charts.

Guitar Audition Charts

The first chart is one that could be used if your guitar auditioners have a song prepared and is intended for a more formal or traditional style of audition. If they didn't cover everything you wanted in the song, ask them about what you want them to cover afterward. Pick the scales you want them to play and a couple of 6th and 5th string barre chords. *Fret board* is intended to gauge the auditioner's knowledge of the notes on the fret board so they can form barre chords and scales without prompting or being given fret numbers.

GUITAR AUDITION CHART - Auditioner's Name: John Dough					
	Chords	Barre Chords	Scales	Fret board	Audition song
Beginning level					
Some knowledge					
Demonstrates skill	X	X	X	X	
Outstanding skill					

Notes: *No audition song. Knows the following chords: C, G, F, A, Em, E, Am.*

This second chart is more of an informal audition chart where the coach is actually playing first, the auditioner is imitating, and there may or may not be a song formally prepared. As well, many times, at the elementary level at least, learners are beginners or have some limited skill. This second method can help you better understand the auditioner's learning habits and gauge whether the learner will be successful or not especially if their skills are limited. It also helps to lower nervousness and stress on the learner's end. With chords, I ask auditioners to form and play that chord if they know it, if not, I tell them just to say "I don't know that one." Typically, the rest of the sections are imitated. It is also important to have them imitate a guitar solo from one of the songs you will be working on that year. Since I do play some guitar, I tend to use this second audition format more often:

GUITAR AUDITION CHART - Auditioner's Name:_____Jonathan Doe_____

Song Prepared: <u>Y</u> or N   if so, what? Sweet Child o' Mine

Chords: <u>C</u>   <u>D</u>   <u>Am</u>   <u>Em</u>   <u>G</u>   <u>A</u>   E   F

Imitation: C, Em, G, D. Did a good job and was able to playback with little guidance.

Barre Chords: Y or <u>N</u>   Power Chords Y or <u>N</u>

Imitation: Was able to imitate the forms really well and move with them.

Scale Patterns: <u>minor pentatonic</u>   <u>blues</u>   major   minor

Imitation: Wasn't familiar with them but was able to imitate me well to get them.

Notes:

Bass

Time required: 6–9 minutes

Minimum Required Skills:

> Pitch names of open strings and/or the note names of a few different *key* frets (fourth string G, third string C, etc.) or very good memory and imitation skills.

> Ability to imitate *Minor Pentatonic Box Pattern* or a minor arpeggio.

Ideal Skills:

> Pitch names for entire fret board for at least the 3rd and 4th strings. At least up to the 7th fret for 1st and 2nd strings.

> **Scale patterns:** minor pentatonic, blues, major, minor.

> Lots of experience learning music by ear and the ability to read tablature and chord charts.

> The ability to "read" guitar chord formations by sight.

Bass Audition Charts

Bass is usually, from what I have noticed, an instrument that many learners know very little about. Many times, they think it is the same thing as a guitar. As we know, they look very similar but are very different. In the amount of time I have been doing this in schools, I have only had a handful of students audition for bass specifically. In the first two years alone, I had one bass player audition. In the past, I have had devoted bass players but typically I will have guitar players double on bass throughout the year especially if no bass players audition. Not only is it extremely common for guitarists to play guitar in one band and bass in another, doubling on bass helps to reinforce the pitch names of the fretboard with young guitar learners and helps them to remember where the root notes of their chords are. Knowing the notes on the fretboard is paramount for bass players and the ability to "read" guitar chords is an asset. I suggest this chart as a place to start with your devoted bass players (next page). *Dexterity* refers to their ability to get around the wider frets of a bass. However, I have also used a chart very similar to the guitar audition chart above, where auditioners were asked to play scales and imitate the coach.

BASS AUDITION CHART – Auditioner's Name:	*Janie Doe*	
	Dexterity	Fretboard Knowledge
Beginning level		
Some Knowledge	X	
Demonstrates Skill		X
Outstanding Skill		

Notes: *Pretty good knowledge of the fretboard. Knew up to the 5th fret on the 3rd and 4th strings.*

Drums

Time Required: 4–7 Minutes

Minimum Required Skills:

Ability to imitate and play a basic rock pattern continuously with a steady beat.

Ideal Skills:

The following grooves: Rock, blues, disco, shuffle, or other and should be able to demonstrate a four-measure phrase with each of them (three measures and a fill).

Rudiments: Basic 5 (see page 51).

Lots of experience with learning music by ear and the ability to understand some rhythm syllables and subdivisions.

Drum Audition Charts

It is important that your band has a good drummer or two. They can really make or break a band. My drum audition charts have evolved into a hybrid chart like the one below. The *Playback* can be omitted if your skills are limited with regard to demonstration. Thus, this chart could easily be used for a formal or informal type of audition. I ask drum auditioners if they have a drum set at home because it is the least likely instrument for students to have at home. If they have one at home it will make it easier for them to practice their repertoire than if they do not. *Grip* refers to the auditioner's preferred grip (ie: matched or traditional) or if they are beginners, their ability to grip the sticks naturally without a pointed finger. *Steady beat* is a four-point rubric with four being the steadiest. The *Patterns played in notation* section is meant for the coach to write down, in short-hand drum notation, what the auditioner played so as to better rate their skill level later. This section of the chart can be used much more effectively for players with limited or little experience. I usually begin with the *experience* section of the audition then ask them to demonstrate what they know if they can. This part can dictate the rest of the audition and can give you all of the information you need. If they are beginners or aren't sure what to do, you can go through each step of the audition chart. *Fills* refers to the auditioner's ability to hear and perform a four-measure phrase with a simple fill and continue the pattern without skipping a beat.

DRUMS AUDITION CHART – Auditioner's Name: _Johnny Doe_

Experience: <u>Y</u> or N   **Drum set at home:** Y or <u>N</u>

Grip: Relaxed and natural

Steady beat: 1   2   3   <u>4</u>

Playback: A quick learner

Patterns: <u>rock</u>   <u>blues</u>   disco   shuffle

Fills: <u>Y</u> or N

Patterns played in notation:

X   X   X   X   X   X   X   X   X X X X X X X X X X X X
        o   o   o   o   o
o   o   o   o   o
Notes:

Keyboard

Time Required: 3–6 minutes

Minimum Required Skills:

The ability to form major and minor triads but diads are also acceptable in many cases.

The ability to figure out, by ear, a major scale or the ability to imitate a major scale or blues scale with good accuracy using both hands separately or together.

Ideal Skills:

The ability to form all chords in all inversions and understand the theory behind them. This means that they should know that in a minor chord, the third is lowered by a half step, or know that voicings of CEG and GCE are the same chords in different inversions.

All major, minor, pentatonic, blues scales, and/or modes that are asked of them.

Lots of experience with learning music by ear and the ability to read chord charts and read some standard music notation.

Keyboard Audition Charts

Many times, keyboard players will have had Royal Conservatory training or some kind of private instruction. Due to this, they tend to understand the theory behind music much more than other musicians in the band and will likely be able to read some standard music notation. However, as we know, reading music is not overly important in this genre of music but can be used as a supplementary tool. I have only utilized this skill a handful of times with my young keyboard players and it is *always* used in combination with listening to the recording. Also, keyboard players are required to prepare an audition song that reflects their abilities on the instrument. Many times they have a private teacher and will be working on something with them anyway. An audition chart should reflect these skills. Here is the chart that I use:

I will write in the scales and chords they can play either in the boxes or in the notes section at the bottom of the chart.

KEYBOARD AUDITION CHART – Auditioner's Name: _Jane Doe_				
	Scales	Blues Scales	Chords	Audition Song
Beginning Level		X		
Some Knowledge	X			
Demonstrates Skill			X	X
Outstanding Skill				

C, G major   C, F, G, Cm, Fm, Gm, D

Notes: Was able to pick up on formula for chord formations quickly.

I always ask them to play major scales with both hands right after their audition song. C, F, and G are good places to start. After this, other guitar-friendly keys like D and A are logical next steps. Then I ask them if they have any experience with blues scales. If they don't, I play them a C minor blues scale (see Chapter 4) and have them copy me. After their scales, I ask them to form major and minor chords. I begin with C then immediately ask them to make it minor. If they are unsure of how to do this then I explain to the auditioner the rule for making a major chord into a minor one by telling them that the 3rd, or 3rd finger, has to move down a half step. Sometimes I will demonstrate if they don't already know what I mean. Once they understand the rule, I ask them to play the following chords to see if they can play them: G, Gm, F, Fm. G and F are typically chords that keyboard players will know if they are taking lessons. Gm and Fm are typically not chords they will know, but, if they know the rule on how to make the chord minor, they will get it very quickly. After this, if the auditioner is doing well, I will ask them to play Em and then to make it major to see if they can either hear the difference or logically know what to do based on their new knowledge.

Vocals

Time Required: 3–5 minutes

Minimum Required Skills:

Ability to sing in-tune without accompaniment.

Good pitch retention.

Ideal Skills:

Impeccable tuning with good projection in all registers.

Outstanding pitch retention.

Vocal Audition Charts

Vocalists are the focal point of the rock band, meaning that the audience will watch and listen to them first, especially if the song that they are singing is one that the audience knows. The auditions for vocalists are the shortest, which is good considering vocal auditions will take up the bulk of your time. These auditions are in two parts. During the first part, they are asked to sing an excerpt of a song of their choice. I usually stop them after about 45 seconds or so as this is usually enough time for me to tell how well they can keep on pitch. The second part is the *Pitch Retention Test.* This test will be the deciding factor for your vocalists. It assesses the auditioner's ability to remember a series of pitches and sing them back accurately. The more accurate, the better! If it comes down to two auditioners whose prepared songs were both amazing, but one did better on the pitch retention test, the one that did better on the test will win the audition. Not only is this a very effective way to gauge the ability or your incoming singers, it is a key indicator of success on this instrument. Here is an example of the charts that I use for the auditions and an example of my pitch retention tests (next page):

VOCAL AUDITION CHART – Auditioner's Name:	John Doe		
	Tuning	Tone Projection	Pitch Retention
Beginning Level			
Some Skill			
Demonstrates Skill	X	X	
Outstanding Skill			X

Song name: Don't Stop Believin'

Notes: Great pitch retention. A little pitchy in places for his solo.

During the pitch retention test, I always start with these four simple melodies. I ask auditioners to sing back what I play on a vowel they are comfortable with. Give an example if they are not sure what is expected.

Pitch Retention 1

Start by playing each measure separately and have the auditioner sing each back. This dictates where to go next.

Pitch Retention 2

If the auditioner gets at least three out of four right in *Pitch Retention 1*, I will move onto the next part of the test:

The second test will really weed out the students with good pitch retention from the ones with *very* good pitch retention. If auditioners are getting all of these, I usually try and extend it a bit more to challenge them. Larger leaps and range extensions are the next logical steps here.

How Many to Take?

Smaller groups are better and more authentic to this genre but rock bands can have as few as three members and as many as 12. From my experience, 12 is the absolute maximum I will take for a single band. After this, management issues arise and making sure everyone is featured becomes more difficult. It is better to have two or three smaller groups because smaller groups can learn music quicker and are relatively easy to manage. Individuals are also forced to make sure they know their parts because they may be the only person on that instrument. I have found that the ideal instrumentation for a school rock band is two to three singers, two guitar players and a bass (three guitar players that share the bass), one to two keyboard players, and one to two drummers per band.

CHAPTER 8

Chapter 8: In Rehearsal

Now that your band has been picked, it's time to decide when to rehearse. In years when we have two rock bands, the rehearsals vary in length and frequency. One band has one 50-minute rehearsal a week after school while the other band rehearses during the day on a pull-out system and meets for 25–30 minutes two to three times in a six-day cycle. This could vary depending on how your school board operates. Another possible rehearsal time is during recess. All three are a very effective use of time but are also extremely different with regard to planning and how the rehearsals will go. The first part of this chapter is a pros and cons list for all options mentioned for you to make the best decision for your school and your program.

After School (50 + minutes once a week)		Pull-Out (two to three times a cycle for 25 or 30 minutes each)		Recess (two or three times a cycle for 25–30 minutes each)	
Pro	**Con**	**Pro**	**Con**	**Pro**	**Con**
Can cover a lot of material due to the extended time.	Learners could be very tired after spending all day in school and therefore lack the focus necessary for the rehearsal.	Can be used as a way to motivate students in regular class work because they sign a contract stating they will keep on top of their missed work.	Flow of rehearsal is interrupted and much time at the beginning of each rehearsal is devoted to review from last rehearsal.	Learners who have given up their recess time a few times a week show that they value being a member of the band.	Those learners who do not value being in the band could begin to show their true colours by choosing to go outside instead of coming to rehearsal.
Can cover more complex concepts due to time.	Learners can more easily forget material if they aren't practicing due to the infrequency of rehearsal time.	If a learner misses a rehearsal, it is easier to make it up.	Less time for songwriting.	Learners will be able to remember material better due to the frequency of the rehearsals.	Attendance can become an issue depending on how often rehearsals happen.
More time each rehearsal can be devoted to songwriting.	If a learner misses a rehearsal, they miss a lot.	Due to frequency of rehearsals, learners will be able to remember material more often.	Learners often arrive late and sporadically depending on their individual class schedules.	Does not disrupt other classes.	For the elementary music coach, this could mean giving up valuable time for preparation and planning.
Students arrive early and ready to go at the designated time because there is usually a small break between their last class and the beginning of rehearsal.	Only a few staff members will hear the band rehearse.	Administration, other staff members, and students can hear the band rehearse which can serve a great PR vehicle for the program.	Pull-out systems often fall victim to standardized test schedules in homeroom classes which seem to fall just before concerts.	Does not need a permission form signed by parents.	Rehearsal flow can be interrupted.
Attendance in general is less of a problem than other formats.	May conflict with after school sports in certain times of the year.		Depending on how the music room is laid out or where it is in the school, this format could disrupt other classes.		May conflict with intramurals depending on how the physical education program operates in your school.

The First Rehearsal

In this section of the chapter, I will be using "You Really Got Me" by the Kinks to take you through what a first rehearsal could look like for a group with little or no experience on their instruments. A band containing musicians with good ears, good by-ear-learning skills, or lots of playing experience will find this song extremely easy and could skip many or all of these steps. The first rehearsal is all about establishing the *groove* for groups of all levels. Not only is *groove* a drumming term, it also refers to the tightness or, for the classically trained musicians, the sense of ensemble or togetherness. For this, the only sheets of paper your young musicians will need are lyric sheets for the singers. The following is a list of steps I go through to help my inexperienced musicians establish groove and learn the parts of the song to performance:

Step 1: Listening

So that we can begin to practice our by-ear-learning process and begin to establish a sense of groove, I have the students actively listen to the song up to the end of the second chorus. Before we do this, I ask them to see if they can pick out their own instrument's parts and focus on them. After we feel like we have a good handle on how the song goes, we try it on the instruments.

Step 2: Learning the Parts

In "You Really Got Me" there are three basic riffs to learn. Here are the guitar, bass, and keyboard parts (see next page):

Riff 1: F–G–G–F–G

If your guitarists have issues with moving their hands in the power chord position quickly, this song works really well by just playing the root notes by following the bass line and letting the keyboard player cover the 5[th]s. However, I will often have the pianist play the root notes only at first just to learn the riffs and then add the 5th in later. I will assume that we are only going to be playing the root notes and therefore will only be concerned with the 6th string frets 1–3–3–1–3 (F–G–G–F–G). We start out slowly, making sure that we are using fingers 1 and 3 (see Chapter 4) and moving them in rhythm. As we play it together, I say the note names with them to help them learn the notes and remember the riffs. Once your guitar players are comfortable with this, the next two riffs will be relatively simple:

Riff 1: You Really Got Me

Riff 2: G-A-A-G-A

Using the same fingering pattern (1–3–3–1–3), the guitar players will simply move up two frets and play the same pattern. We will repeat this a few times until they are comfortable again before moving on to the third and final riff. I will say the note names as we play them again:

Riff 2: You Really Got Me

You Really Got Me
Words and Music by Ray Davies Copyright (c) 1964 Jayboy Music Corp.
Copyright Renewed
This arrangement Copyright (c) 2017 Jayboy Music Corp.
All Rights Administered by Sony/ATV Music Publishing LLC, 424 Church Street, Suite 1200, Nashville, TN 37219
International Copyright Secured All Rights Reserved
Reprinted by permission of Hal Leonard LLC

Riff 3: C–D–D–C–D

Again, using the same fingering and melodic pattern, the riff moves up one **string** this time to the 5th string. The same learning strategy is repeated until they are comfortable:

Riff 3: You Really Got Me

You Really Got Me
Words and Music by Ray Davies Copyright (c) 1964 Jayboy Music Corp.
Copyright Renewed
This arrangement Copyright (c) 2017 Jayboy Music Corp.
All Rights Administered by Sony/ATV Music Publishing LLC, 424 Church Street, Suite 1200, Nashville, TN 37219
International Copyright Secured All Rights Reserved
Reprinted by permission of Hal Leonard LLC

Step 3: Adding Drums

Depending on your group, drums could have been going the entire time the band was getting used to each riff. This helps your musicians begin to feel the groove early on. Or, drums could be added after the riffs have been learned. Each method is effective and will be different for every group of learners you have. For this, drummers will play a basic rock pattern (see page 49). For the purposes of being able to feel the groove, drummers will begin to play their pattern without the rest of the band. Once the drummer(s) have established a consistent, steady rock pattern, add in the guitar/keyboard riff beginning with *Riff 1*. Learners may notice from the recording that guitars begin the song before the drums come in. This is true, but at this point, not important because the focus is on establishing the band's groove. Once they have established a tight groove with the drums using *Riff 1*, explain to the guitar/keyboard players that you will be asking them to switch between each riff smoothly while they are playing.

Step 4: Switching Between Each Riff

At this point, learners will be practicing switching between each riff. It shouldn't be too difficult for most learners but it is an important step. We begin by, again, establishing the groove with *Riff 1*. After this, I say "switch"—this is their cue to switch to *Riff 2*. When they are settled in with *Riff 2*, I ask them to switch again to *Riff 3* this time. It doesn't matter how many times they repeat the riff, the focus during this step is switching smoothly between each one.

Step 5: Active Listening and "Ghosting"

Now it's time to start playing the song as it is on the recording. We listen to the song again to see if we can hear where the guitar part switches riffs. Ask them specifically to listen for the switches. Then, we try it all together with a technique called *ghosting*. *Ghosting* is where we all play together but we play along with the recording without any volume. Guitars and keyboards will turn all the way down and the drummers will *air drum*, meaning they will play their part but not hit any drums. This is where electronic drums would come in handy. If you have a set of electronic drums, have them play those without any sound. Singers should sing along with their lyric sheets without their microphones.

Explain to learners that they are going to try to play their parts along with the recording without any volume and see if they can put all the switches in the right place. They may feel quick to your musicians so working to build the tempo before trying it with the recording may be needed. In any case, it will show them how fast they need to play and will exercise their muscles to be able to play it up to tempo. Only ghost up to the end of the first chorus for now.

Step 6: Singers and Putting it All Together

Turn everything back up and try it all together. Ask the guitar and keyboard players to see if they can switch in the right place while we play this time. Sometimes, to start out, I will play the guitar part with them and help them along with the switches. Many times, learners will be able to sense the switches on their own. Start with *Riff 1* and cue the singers when the groove is established. If singers need to hear the melody again, this would be a good place to stop and listen to the song again. Once they get going, play up to the end of the first chorus.

Step 7: Adding in the Tag

There is a short and easy two-measure phrase at the end of every chorus to transition back into the verse called a *tag*. If you feel like your musicians have a good grasp of *Step 6* after going through it a couple of times, it will be time to add in this two-measure tag to complete the first third of the song:

The Tag

From chorus   To verse

This is known as a *tag* because it is tagged on at the end of the chorus. Try getting your musicians to play it in context once they have it learned.

At this point, it is important to tell your learners that they now know the entire song. They will be shocked. They just have to do what they just learned three times! One of the verses even has the same lyrics. This entire process from Steps 1 through 7 should take 30 to 40 minutes for even a beginner group. The only homework I assign to them is to listen to the song as much as possible every night. They don't even have to actively listen, they just have to put it in their ears a couple of times a night. The reason we all remember lyrics and melodies to the songs we hear on the radio is because we hear them on the radio constantly. See Chapter 6 for more on *passive listening*.

Subsequent Rehearsals

In our second rehearsal, we will typically review the parts we learned in the previous one and then play through the entire song. Beforehand, listen to the song as a group and ghost as best you can. If the learners have done their homework, this will come together quite quickly. The only aspect that might be a challenge is the tempo in this song and I will typically not add the guitar solo at this time. It is not important that the tempo be as bright as the recording at this point either. A steady groove, however, is paramount even if it's a little slow. Your musicians should be able to get through the entire song but remember to leave room for the guitar solo after the second chorus. This will be discussed later.

The Ending

After the song's final chorus comes the ending (see next page).

The Ending

You Really Got Me
Words and Music by Ray Davies Copyright (c) 1964 Jayboy Music Corp.
Copyright Renewed
This arrangement Copyright (c) 2017 Jayboy Music Corp.
All Rights Administered by Sony/ATV Music Publishing LLC, 424 Church Street, Suite 1200, Nashville, TN 37219
International Copyright Secured All Rights Reserved
Reprinted by permission of Hal Leonard LLC

The Missing Parts

Some of your musicians, depending on their level, may have added in the extra back-up vocal parts and the other keyboard part. This is okay, it means that they have been listening carefully to the song and likely did more than just passive listening for homework. This is a natural occurrence when learning this type of music. If they are shy, they may ask if they can add in the part they were hearing instead of doing it without prompting. This is okay too! Just let it happen.

The Solo

If your learners wanted to try and learn the guitar solo on the recording by ear, this is also okay. However, I typically have my musicians improvise a solo in G minor pentatonic. See Chapter 4 for a review on the *pentatonic box pattern* (page 42). Just use that pattern but start on the 3rd fret (G). This is also a great way to rotate through the band to give everyone a chance to improvise a solo. Many times, depending on the skill level of my musicians, I go over the scale pattern with everybody and assign it for homework so when they come back they have a pretty good idea of how to play the scale pattern and can move it around to play in any key. Less is more with improvised solos, too many notes can often sound boring and contrived. Get your musicians to keep it simple by choosing three or four notes in the middle of the pattern with plenty of *string bends.* See Chapter 6 for review on string bends (page 84).

Now that all the parts are put together, rehearse as you see fit. The next section discusses other considerations you might come across while rehearsing your groups.

Transposing

This song can be easily transposed if need be. I try to keep songs in their original key as much as possible. However, there are times when you might have to transpose a song up or down a step. Going beyond a step in either direction can hurt the integrity of the song and make some instruments' parts more difficult. However, here are some reasons you might want to transpose a song:

- **It makes the song easier to play**
    - If transposing by a step puts your song in an easier key to play for everyone, it should be considered. For example, if the song is in the key of A but playing it in G would make the song easier to play, you should do it.
- **It is easier on the singers**
    - One of the main reasons to transpose is for the sake of the singers. This could be the only case where you might transpose by more than a step, but only if the other instrument parts are not made more difficult. For example, if the song is originally in C and transposing it by more than a step would put your instrumentalists in E♭ or F, this should be avoided.
- **The guitars are in down tunings**
    - Songs in down tunings might as well be transposed up a step because playing them in the original key would mean down tuning (see page 35) all the guitars before playing that song. Typically, bands that have songs in down tunings perform all their songs that way. *Audacity*, as

mentioned earlier, is a great free app for transposing the recording up a step so your musicians can practice with the recording at home.

- **The song can be transposed without learning anything new**
  - If the song can be transposed by just moving a form up or down without learning anything new, transposing could be considered. A great example of this is the song we just learned, "You Really Got Me" by The Kinks. There are no real chords played in the entire song. Transposing it up a step is incredibly easy because instead of starting on frets 1–3–3–1–3, your learners would start on 3–5–5–3–5 and continue the pattern from there. The keyboard parts are easily transposed here too. Both the original key and up a step include no sharps or flats in those parts. Most songs with only power chords or only barre chords can be easily transposed for guitar because the only change would be the fret number.
- **There are always capos and many times, transpose buttons**
  - Capos can be used to instantly transpose a song up for guitar without changing anything but the pitch. Hand positions and chord forms stay exactly the same. Transpose buttons on keyboards can be used in this manner too.

Tuning the Guitars

You could tune the guitars before every rehearsal, or you could let your learners figure out how to do it. In Chapter 4 I introduce you to the guitar and the open string pitches. There are two main ways to help students understand tuning a stringed instrument and how to tune a stringed instrument. Each have their own benefits and drawbacks:

- **With the help of the keyboard players**
  - With this method, guitar players work with the keyboard player(s), one at a time, to tune each guitar separately using their ears. Each pitch is played on the keyboard first and then the guitarist plays that pitch to try and match it as closely as they can. They don't move onto the next string until the pitch is matched. The keyboard players will need some guidance as to what pitches to play at first but will soon catch on. The goal is to get rid of as many "wobbles" in the sound as they can. Here is a pros and cons list for this method of tuning guitars:

Pros	Cons
Everyone in the band gets to try and help tune the guitars either directly or passively through listening.	Takes a long time to go through every guitar player in the band but over time it does get faster as learners get better at hearing the pitches.
The keyboard players know the names of the open strings on the guitar and bass.	Learners will always need another person to help them tune.
Challenges many members to hear extremely close pitch tolerances.	The piano has inherent "wobbles" on single pitches even when in tune caused by the way the instrument is traditionally tuned and built.
Helps to train the ears of every member in the band.	Difficult to tune on the fly because this method needs complete silence.

- **Using a clip-on tuner, built-in tuner, or tuning pedal**
  - Clip-on tuners, built-in tuners, and tuning pedals are the most accurate way to tune guitars. Clip-on tuners literally clip onto the head stock of the guitar and pick up the vibrations from the instrument to accurately gauge pitch. Built-in tuners are usually in the guitar amplifier. Chapter 3 discusses gear and mentions the **Mustang** series of **Fender** amplifiers. These are just one line of amplifiers with built-in tuners. The tuning function can be accessed by the push of a button. Tuning pedals are sold separately and can be plugged into the amplifier and then into the guitar and are activated by pressing the switch with the guitar player's foot. All of these tuners do not need sound from the amplifier. This opens a wide range of benefits for the coach and the learners. One of

the biggest benefits of this is that learners will be able to tune guitars on their own which will save you valuable time in rehearsal and performance.

Pros	Cons
Once learners know how to use the tuners, it is an extremely quick way to tune guitars.	Not everyone is involved in helping tune the guitars.
It is very accurate.	The skill of distinguishing between extremely close pitch tolerances is not practiced.
Works with other sounds and noises in the room meaning they can tune while everyone else is warming up.	Keyboard players don't learn the names of the open strings on the guitar.
Learners become accustomed to what *in tune* sounds like quicker.	
Tuning in the middle of songs or on the fly is easy.	
Learners will be able to quickly check the tuning before a performance without any guidance.	

Wrapping Cables

Wrapping cables properly is an underappreciated skill that many people do not realize they are doing wrong. I get my singers to set up and put away their microphones every rehearsal. This means that they get to learn how to use the mixer on a basic level and how to properly wrap their cables. Regardless of how long it takes, this skill should be practiced after every rehearsal so that, at the very least, you will have two or three students who can help you with set up and tear-down at concert time. Also, learning to wrap cables properly is a directly useful skill in this discipline. It is also a good idea to have your guitar players wrap their cables up after a rehearsal so that they can help with set up and tear-down too. Having cable clips or wraps will be very helpful for when you are setting up as well. These prevent the cables from getting damaged or tangled together during set up.

Steps to wrapping a cable properly:

STEP ONE

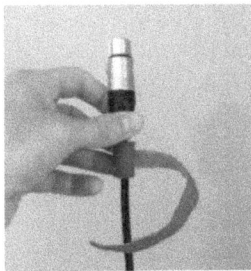

First, get one of these cable clips. They will be extremely handy later on.

STEP TWO

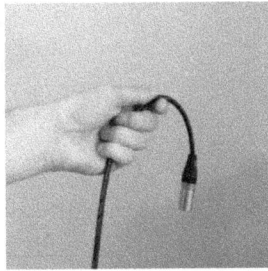

Then hold the cable in your left hand as above.

STEP THREE

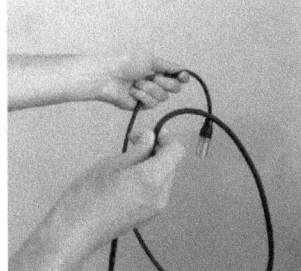

Then, using your right hand and fingers, twist the cable so that it forms a perfect circle as in the next picture. It usually gets tangled during a performance or rehearsal. Twisting as you form it will get rid of the tangles.

STEP FOUR

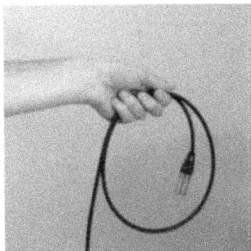

STEP FIVE

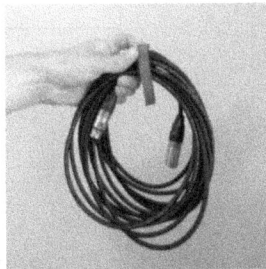

Keep forming circles using these steps until you have this.

STEP SIX

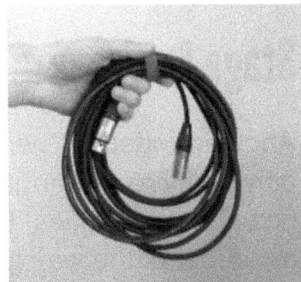

Continued on next page…

After following these steps, close the clip to neatly store the cable in a tote or box.

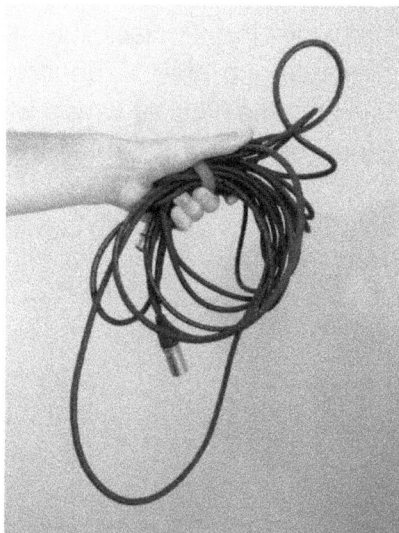

If your cables look like this then you did something wrong. Go back to the beginning.

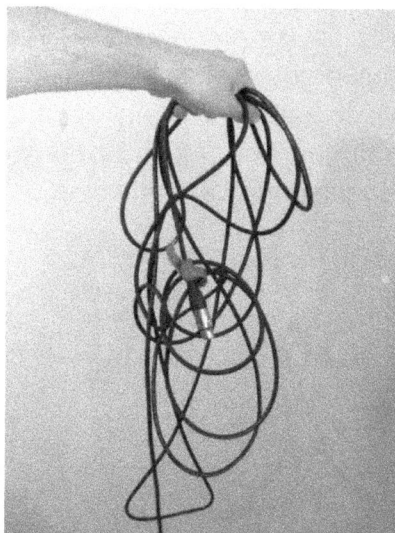

If you follow all these steps but don't use the cable clip, this is what will happen when you take it out of the box again.

Stage Presence

Another aspect of performance to consider is stage presence. For me, this doesn't only apply to the ability to command a stage, it also refers to showing the audience how the music goes. For example, if the guitar player has a solo, having the singers move out of the way and the guitarist with the solo move forward is a simple but very effective trick to enhance a performance. This simple action not only helps the audience understand who is playing, it looks extremely professional and brings the calibre of the performance up automatically. If the focus shifts to a young musician on a stationary instrument like a piano or drum kit, simply having the singers gesture to that person can be very effective. This is why having your horn players use wireless clip-on microphones is important because they will need to step to the front for solos.

CHAPTER 9

Chapter 9: Creativity and Songwriting

Since I have started playing guitar, I've noticed that it's one of those instruments with which a person can easily be drawn into composing and improvising. I have dabbled in a bit of composition and songwriting with my guitar, but my problem is that I know too much and tend to over-think and analyze what I'm doing. Children do not have any of the inhibitions of a trained musician.[14]

Children's Inherent Creativity[§]

In a TEDTalks by creativity advocate and scholar Sir Ken Robinson, he mentioned that children from a very young age are not afraid to be wrong. If they don't know, they "just give it a go"[15]—they improvise. Unfortunately, he says, creativity is educated out of us pretty early on. We become too well 'trained.' He points out that "if you're not prepared to be wrong, you will never come up with anything original." I am a prime example of this, I have more years of training to be a musician than these kids have been alive and they seem to have songwriting figured out! There have been many school rock bands in separate years that have written and performed their own songs. One band had their song, "Don't Go," recorded and can be heard at this address:
http://stevesmusicroom.WebStarts.com/uploads/Don_t_Go_-_A_C_R_.mp3
I was impressed, every time a group composed a song together, by how simple but well-thought-out the songs were. The band this past year didn't get a chance to record their song but the writing process they went through to performance was really quite remarkable. It was done in the same way that my band, The Sidewalks, write our songs, except that it happened much more efficiently. Here is how it worked with a school band from a couple of years ago:

> ... because they don't have all the training that I have had, they just do what sounds good ...

One of the guitarists came to rehearsal one day with a very circular, four-measure chord progression. He showed the progression to the other guitarists in the band and the drummers started to play a groove. One of the singers, who was in Grade 4 at the time, started singing a melody almost instantaneously as if she had done it before. Her melody was really catchy and the rest of the band was immediately hooked. Within about 20 minutes of just jamming out the new song, we had workable lyrics for a verse, a possible progression for a chorus and even a guitar solo! It really came together quite quickly, with very little guidance from me. All of this was able to happen because I facilitated an environment of trial and error so that students could feel safe improvising with their peers. At the same time, because they don't have all of the training that I have had, they *just do what sounds good* and have very few inhibitions because they are not analyzing and theorizing.

[§] Much of this section was previously published in Canadian Music Educator volume 55, issue 2, pp. 44–46.

Rock Bands are Conducive to Students Writing Their Own Music

As mentioned earlier in the book, playing in rock bands is naturally conducive to learners writing their own songs. In the current classical music world, musician and composer are generally separated from each other; they do not interact. In the rock music world, there is no separation; musicians and composers are one and the same much like it was in the classical world during the time of Mozart and many of the other greats. Somewhere along the line, this was lost. Rock music never had that separation. The main reason for this is because rock musicians are not bound by particular methods or notation like in classical or jazz and typically learn their instrument without the coaching of another person. As we've learned in Chapter 6, this is completely normal, authentic to the genre, and an aspect of rock music that needs to be preserved to keep the creative nature of rock music alive. As a musician who has performed in all genres from classical to rock, I have never felt more creative than when I was in rock groups. Even as much as jazz musicians are considered the ultimate improvisers and creators, they are still bound by the way the greats of jazz used to do it and many times the separation of musician and composer still exists. In rock music, musician and composer are one-in-the-same. There is no separation. Also, there are no limitations and no *wrong* ways of doing things, nor should there be. Here is an example of what I mean: I remember a particular time when one of my school rock groups was writing their own song. We all agreed on a chord progression and the keyboard player began to play it on her own to start the song. At one point, instead of playing an Em chord, she played an E major chord by *mistake*. The E major chord did not belong to the key we were in but it sounded good and really made the chord progression stick. We tried both progressions, one with the Em and one with the E, and they all agreed that the progression with the E major chord sounded better—so we kept it. Many of history's greatest discoveries and greatest songs were inspired by, or sprouted from, a *mistake*.

> Many of history's greatest discoveries and greatest songs were inspired by, or sprouted from, a *mistake*.

Songwriting With Your Young Rockers

Songwriting is a natural extension of playing rock music. Most of the time, it will happen with very little or no coaching. All you need to do as the coach is set up a safe environment for making mistakes and trying new things. Many times, students will be songwriting at home and have ideas to take back to rehearsal already. Sometimes they will need a bit of guidance to get started. If they do need a bit of guidance, I begin by using the following chart:

Major Scale Chords

	I	ii	iii	IV	V	vi	♭VII
Key of C	C	Dm	Em	F	G	Am	B♭
Key of G	G	Am	Bm	C	D	Em	F
Key of D	D	Em	F#m	G	A	Bm	C
Key of A	A	Bm	C#m	D	E	F#m	G
Key of E	E	F#m	G#m	A	B	C#m	D
Key of B	B	C#m	D#m	E	F#	G#m	A

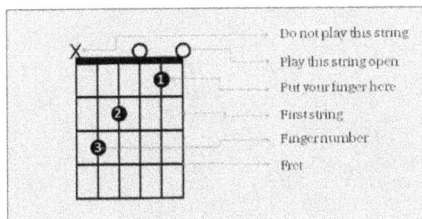

Do not play this string
Play this string open
Put your finger here
First string
Finger number
Fret

The vii chord is diminished (vii°) in every major key but is rarely used. ♭VII is an altered chord that doesn't belong to a major key but is more common than the vii° chord.

This chart shows the chords in the six most common keys for guitar. If your musicians don't already have a chord progression figured out, they can use this chart to get them started. All they do is pick a key from the chart and go from there. They can pick as little as one chord or as many as six. I would suggest three or four to begin with. Then we jam them out together. What I mean by this is, everyone plays the progression together, the drums come in with a pattern that fits and the singers try to improvise melodies. Some groups may take a while to get started but generally you won't even need to talk about improvising or how do to it, especially with singers. They just, as Ken Robinson says, "give it a go." They may impress you.

Three things to note about this chart:

1. This is only intended to be a place to start or to generate ideas, so if your musicians use a chord that is in a different key but it still sounds good, use it. These are called altered chords.

2. This chart shows the $\flat VII$ chord for each key instead of the diminished vii chord that is normally on the 7th scale degree. This is because, in this style, diminished vii chords are rarely used but the $\flat VII$ chord is used quite often. Historically it was used in blues and has become a widely used altered chord in many rock tunes.

3. Setting too many rules for your musicians can hinder their creativity. I always try and include the I chord in songs to establish key but if your musicians use chords within a key that does not include the I chord, it's okay. Songs can begin to sound the same if you try to establish key. I am not saying that establishing a key isn't important, because it is, I am simply saying that worrying about theory will hinder your musicians' ability to come up with something new. Key can be established later when improvising a solo or coming up with a melody. Or they can learn many theoretical concepts through composing first.

Purchasing this book automatically gives you free access to the *Major Scale Chords* chart. If you would like a poster size file of the *Major Scale Chords Chart,* please contact me at steve@stevesmusicroom.com and let me know you purchased a copy of the book. You can then use the file to print your own copy at most printing companies.

Song Form

Due to the relatively simple form of most rock songs, all they need is a verse, chorus, and a bridge. I always tell them that the verse and chorus can sound similar but the bridge can sound completely different. A typical rock song will have the following form:

Verse [Verse] →*Chorus*→*Verse*→*Chorus*→*Bridge*→*[Verse]*→*Chorus*→*Chorus*

The verses will have the same melody for the most part but different lyrics. The Chorus is usually the same every time and is the part of the song that most people know because they hear it more often than the verses. The bridge can be anything from an a cappella chorus, a rap, to a guitar solo, or anything else that your musicians might be able to come up with. A perfect example of this form is "Take on Me" by A Ha! You and your learners will notice a pattern to how pop and rock songs are written once you realize this form.

Many times singers in these rock groups seem to have a knack for writing lyrics. Lyrics are an aspect of songwriting that I struggle with personally so letting my learners explore this is simple: I let them take the lead. My over-thinking and over-analyzing doesn't get in the way here. Usually, the lyrics are quite good and only need minor tweaks or revisions. The best part is they are usually willing to write them down on the spot or take them home to work on them after rehearsal. I have a technique for generating lyric ideas that will be discussed in the next chapter. Also in the next chapter is a section called *Songwriting as a Class Project*, which will discuss a class project I did with my learners where they wrote songs, arranged them in their regular music classes and performed them in concert.

Improvising

Improvising is often described as *spontaneous composition* but I find that this description makes it sound too formalized. Improvising is much more approachable if it is thought of as experimenting with or creating musical ideas. Musical ideas can be four beats long or four measures long and thinking of it this way gets rid of the stigma surrounding improvisation of having to compose a coherent melody on the spot. Improvisations only become compositions when they are either written down or recorded. For example, in the recording studio, many times, those epic *improvised* guitar solos that could not have possibly been improvised on the spot were not improvised on the spot! That 30-second clip of a solo in many cases was played and recorded up to ten times, ten different ways and then cut up and spliced together to make a coherent composition. Then, many times, that musician in that band simply learns the recorded solo and that is what they perform in concert. This being said, there are bands with musicians who do actually improvise that epic solo in the first take.

Improvising in rock ensembles is paramount. Everyone in the band should have opportunities to be creative. Stigma around improvisation, especially in jazz, dictates that they must compose complex music on the spot in the style of whatever composer happened to write the tune without any mistakes. This is a poor way to learn and to think about improvisation. Improvisation can simply be coming up with an idea and trying it out. An example of this would be asking a learner to find a simple two-beat drum fill that works and trying it. It can be as basic as teaching your guitar player the first five notes of a scale and having them play around with them. It could be having your singers embellish a melody to fit their personal style. The options are endless. In this regard, improvisation is not taught, it is experienced and learned through doing. If you open it up, small embellishments, added parts, and improvisations will occur naturally.

Improvisation and by-ear-learning is the ability, essentially, to speak music. Here is a quote that sums up my thoughts on improvisation: "The capacities for creative self-expression and spontaneous conversational interaction indicate a person's proficiency in the use of a verbal language. The most exactly equivalent music skill is that of improvisation".[16] In other words, you should learn to *speak* the language of music (learning by ear, improvising, creating) before you learn to write it. A person **never** learns to write a language before they learn to speak it. Children have at least three years of learning how to use the language at home before they learn anything about how to write it. Music is the same and rock music has been teaching kids how to *speak* music long before many of you reading this book were conceived.

Ways to Encourage and Nourish Improvising and Creativity with Your Rock Groups

1. Give opportunities for songwriting every rehearsal or music class.
2. Embrace *mistakes.*
3. Let singers embellish as long as they are the only ones singing. If they are in a group, they should each agree to sing it a certain way.
4. Let drummers come up with their own fills.
5. Teach a minor pentatonic scale to your guitar players but tell them to only pick three pitches to use with a solo.
6. Hold jam sessions at the beginning of every rehearsal where an app plays a chord progression and everyone gets a chance to solo. *Mosh* your solos if

learners are finding it nerve wracking. *Moshing* a solo means everyone solos at the same time.

7. Have students make musical choices about the music.
8. Come up with a new ending for the song if the one on the recording doesn't work.
9. Rearrange a song.
10. Let your musicians find a way to simplify a part that does not take away the integrity of the music.
11. Add a part to a song.
12. Add a harmony to the vocal line.

Much of these will occur naturally without your coaching and some may ask before they do it. Just embrace these moments.

NOTE: Playing songs exactly as they are on the recording is not creative. In this case, you would be making music together—not creating it.

CHAPTER 10

Chapter 10: Including More of the School in Rock Music

Most of what I have told you has been for extracurricular or auditioned bands. However, there is a way to implement this into your regular music classroom to form a classroom band! What is important here is learning the music as rock musicians would learn a song in real life. This chapter will explore how to learn a song in the classroom using the *by-ear-learning* process and then I will guide you through to a performance or *informance*. Here is how I do this:

Introduction

I begin by choosing a very simple song with a repetitive riff. For the purposes of this section, I will be using the song "Lean on Me" by Bill Withers as it has a very repetitive riff and is a widely familiar song.

The *By-Ear-Learning* Process

Before the First Note

Before the learners even touch the instruments, I have them figure out what instruments are in the song. Many of your younger learners will find this step difficult as they have likely never listened to anything other than the singing in their lives. I explain that much like their eyes can focus on a particular word or letter in a book, their ears can focus on a particular sound within a song. They just have to practice it. How I begin is by having them focus on the beginning where there is no singing and ask them to tell me what instruments they think they hear. They always tell me *piano*, and *bass*. Some tell me *guitar* even if they don't hear it at all. This is perhaps because they assume that it includes guitar as most songs from that era do include a guitar, or because they want to play guitar. If I get the answer *guitar*, we listen to it again to make sure and I ask other students about what they hear (there is no guitar at the beginning of this song).

Once we have all the instruments we need (piano and keyboard) we write them on the board and continue listening to when the singing comes in. There is humming right after the first phrase in the music. This is where it gets difficult for some learners because, as mentioned, they have little practice listening to anything else but the vocal line. Therefore, before we start this part I have to tell them to ignore the singing at all costs and keep trying to follow the piano part. To help them be successful, I have them practice this *selective* listening by closing their eyes and trying to focus on the undermusic (a Lucy Green term), meaning the music that is under the vocal line. Closing their eyes aids them in focusing on listening without any visual distractions and can sometimes be helpful in a situation like this. As we go through the song I ask the learners if they hear any new instruments. If you find that learners are having difficulty hearing all the different instruments and parts to the song have them *airplay* or *mimic* the particular part you want them to hear. When you are airplaying you are pretending to play the instrument in the air like *air guitar.* For example, often learners will find it difficult to hear the strings sound in the chorus, if you airplay the violin at that section in the exact same way it is being played on the recording, you will notice that students are able to hear it much better. They attach the action to the sound. Once you and your learners have gotten through the entire song in this way, then you are ready for *The First Note*.

The First Note

My classroom has a number of Orff mallet percussion instruments. We use these instruments to learn the main riff of the song because these instruments are easy to play without any prior training aside from learning how to hold the mallets properly. As an added bonus, the pitch names are etched directly onto the bars of the instruments. These instruments are perfect for learning how the song goes mostly because learners can freely try and figure out how the song is played without technique or remembering note names getting in the way.

I begin the *by-ear-learning* process by having learners figure out the first pitch of the riff only. To give students a chance to be successful, I begin by explaining that to be able to learn it by ear they have to be able to sing the pitch they are hearing so they can match that pitch with their instruments. I play the first chord of the recording without going onto the next section of the song so that all they hear is the first sound of the recording in isolation. The first chord of "Lean on Me" is a C major chord played on the piano. The sound of the C is quite clear and students are able to hear the C in the chord most times. At this time it is not important that the first chord is made up of three different pitches, what is important is that they are trying to listen and play using trial and error. If they are having trouble finding it, I play it on the piano or guitar and have them sing it back to me. Playing it on an instrument in their range helps learners to displace the octave if they need to. At this point, I give them two or three minutes to experiment with what that starting note might be. Every 30 seconds or so I have them sing it so they don't lose the pitch in their ears. The pattern should always be *listen-sing-play*. This part of the process may take up to 10 minutes before we come to a consensus on what the starting pitch is. It could also be as little as three minutes.

Piecing it Up

Once the starting pitch is established, we try and learn the rest of the riff. I only play the opening part of the riff for them and pause it after it returns to the next C (two full measures). Their job at this point is to figure out this part of the song only. As a facilitator, I travel around the room listening to students use trial and error to figure out how it goes. Some students will need some coaching through this process. It is important, that as facilitator I don't show them how to play it. Many students will be tempted to watch other learners play it. Although this is a very legitimate and authentic learning process for this type of music, they should be encouraged to learn the song on their own. This way, learners internalize the process and as discussed earlier, are able to remember it much better. There comes a time when about half of the students will have the part learned and the other half have it very close. Many times, I will help them all get it right as a group because we cannot move onto the next two-measure section of the song until we all know the first part.

This process is repeated until every two-measure section of the riff is learned. After they are all learned, we try and put it together as a class and play it all in unison, seeing if they can loop the entire riff like on the recording. This part of the learning process from first note to playing the entire riff by ear is the longest, but it is extremely valuable for your learners.

Reinforcing Aural Skills

By Grade 3 at my school, I have students writing down multi-measure pentatonic melodies by ear. This means by Grade 5, when forming class bands like the one mentioned above is more common, they have the skills they need to be coached through writing down riffs on a staff. This is an important process because it gives those learners who are having issues with playing the riff a visual to help guide them. By the time we are ready to write we already know the pitches and can perform the riff pretty closely. First, we write out all the pitches in the first few measures before adding rhythms. Then we go beat by beat and measure by measure discussing what rhythm should be attached to each pitch. This song in particular presents a perfect opportunity to discuss ties. As I write it on the board, students write it down on their staved lapboards. We keep going through it until it looks like this:

Lean On Me
Words and Music by Bill Withers
Copyright (c) 1972 INTERIOR MUSIC CORP.
Copyright Renewed
This arrangement Copyright (c) 2017 INTERIOR MUSIC CORP.
All Rights Controlled and Administered by SONGS OF UNIVERSAL, INC.
All Rights Reserved Used by Permission
Reprinted by permission of Hal Leonard LLC

If you choose to forgo the step of writing it down, that is fine. If you decide to do it, however, it should be done *after* most of the learning has been done by ear. This concept reinforces the sound before symbol mantra and if you recall from Chapter 6, no one ever learns a language by first learning how to write it down—they learn it by ear and through imitation. The writing comes after imitation and by-ear-learning is well established.

Chords

The riff in "Lean on Me" is composed of chords in parallel motion. Because of this, learners are able to pick up the concept of chords and parallel motion really well. I divide students into three groups. Each group begins the riff on a different chord tone. Group 1 is all the root notes so they begin on C exactly like they already learned. Group 2 is in charge of the 3rd of the chord so they begin on E and do the exact same pattern. Group 3 begins the riff starting on G. Since learners are using Orff instruments at this time, the pitches that aren't being used in their groups can be taken off.

Another way to do this is to pair learners up on the same instruments and have them begin on different chord tones. I have also had some students play the chord or two different chord tones on their own so they can see how there is always one note in between the root and the 3rd that isn't played.

The Next Step

Once the main riff is established, learners must prove that they know the part on the mallet instruments so they can move to an instrument of their choice to learn the rest of the song. Many of my learners choose drums, keyboard, and electric guitar. Often, we will also have a group of boomwhackers, bells, or various other percussion instruments. The last instrument we add is the vocals, so there would be no one switching to singing at this point. Sometimes I will hold mini-auditions for students who feel like they are ready to move to the next instrument. I usually limit the number of learners switching in the first class to five especially if there are a number of different instruments to get started. Since the students already know how to play the song on one instrument, learning it by ear on the next one is much easier. I usually give them the first pitch because unlike the Orff percussion instruments, the pitch names are not written on the instrument in most cases. If the learner chooses guitar, I have them play the easy versions of the three main chords to the song which in this case are C, F, C, G^7. G will also work instead of G^7. If a particular learner hadn't played guitar before, I use this time to show them how to play these chords. F can be difficult even with a simplified form so starting with C and G^7 might be your best option if your guitar players are beginners. If they like, your learners could try and learn the same riff they learned from the mallet percussion instruments instead of the chords. The pianos play the riff as it is on the recording as best they can by playing in parallel 3rds or triads. Root notes are fine here too. If drummers can execute a pretty good basic rock groove, I have them do that. If they are not quite to that point yet, I have them leave out the hi-hat for the first while and just play the bass drum and snare drum. After all of this, there will likely still be a few students who want to stay on the mallet instruments. This is completely fine and will add a unique timbre to the song. Over the next couple of weeks, we work toward getting everyone on an instrument they would like to perform the song with, while practicing keeping all our parts together.

Arranging

Once learners have their parts learned on their new instruments, we practice putting it together with everything but the singing. At this time, it is a perfect opportunity for learners to rearrange the music. This is as simple as deciding which instrument starts and which one comes in next. Each class doing this song will have a different arrangement of their own. When all the parts are going well together and learners have decided on an arrangement for the introduction that they like, we can add singers. Before the singing is attempted, the singers should have a lyric sheet and the entire band should listen to the song a couple of more times. I usually have them listen to the song in class a couple of times and then ask them to listen to it at least two times at home. Once the singers are added, it comes together quite quickly. For the section of the song that reads "You just call on me brother...", known as the bridge, I have the singers sing this part while the rest of the class plays a *stomp-clap* pattern until the rest of the band comes back in. At the end of the song, we discuss ways to end the song that makes sense. As mentioned, opportunities for arranging and composing present themselves regularly when learning and performing rock music.

Performance/Informance

Once we have practiced our new arrangement a couple of times, I ask learners if they feel like they are ready to perform. Many times they know whether or not they are ready to perform, but occasionally, they will need some guidance on what *performance-ready* sounds like. The performances are pretty informal. Instead of taking all of our gear down to the gymnasium for a professional style performance, we invite classes to come to the music room to hear us play. I like to call these low-key performances *informances*. Most teachers and students are really excited to be invited to hear the *informance*. As well, it is an amazingly easy way to promote your program to the rest of the school and your learners will absolutely love showing off what they can do.

For the first performance, I will occasionally play the song with them. Depending on your group, there will be some learners who will be able to play through the song without you. This is ideal because then they begin to rely on each other instead of their coach. When we perform it a second or third time, I will usually expect learners to be able to perform it without me.

After we have performed it at least once, I give students the choice to switch to a new instrument again. The only catch is that the student who is switching to another instrument must first teach the new part to the person replacing them. Imitation is also an authentic learning practice of popular musicians so doing this will not take away from their experience. As well, the person teaching the part will have to understand it better than the learner and so this is beneficial for both learners. Once we switch again, we will work up to another *informance,* and in every subsequent *informance* learners will be given another opportunity to switch again. Like many rock musicians in the real world, they will have experience playing two or more instruments in the band for the same song.

The entire process from beginning to the first informance should take from September to the end of October or early November. It may seem like this is a long time to be working on one song but the *process* is the focus. It is extremely worthwhile for the learners to go through the *by-ear-learning* process so that they can begin to be comfortable with the strategies to do it on their own. They don't seem to mind working on the same song for this long either because they are either on a different instrument or showing someone how to play it on a new instrument. It is important that this be done without a fixed performance date so that we don't fall into *rehearsal mode* as many of us do just before a formal concert. Doing informances when they are ready is much more beneficial and much less stressful for the learners and the facilitators. That being said, this does not mean that the classroom band cannot be featured in a formal performance. The right amount of time just needs to be budgeted to get the educational value out of this process.

Songs That Work Well Using This Process

Here are some songs that can be very easily used with this process due to their repetitive riffs, and there are many more songs that have repetitive riffs that you may want to use. Songs with a lot of chords and pitches are much more difficult to pick up for learners that are new to by-ear-learning. Most of these songs can be found in the *Song List* in Chapter 5.

"Lean on Me" by Bill Withers
"Stompa" by Serena Ryder
"Eye of the Tiger" by Survivor (Great song to talk about accidentals)
"Stand by Me" by Ben E. King
"You Really Got Me" by The Kinks
"All Day and All of the Night" by The Kinks

"Louie, Louie" by the Kingsmen
"I Love Rock n' Roll" by Joan Jett

Songwriting as a Class Project

As a precursor to this project I'm about to describe, you should know that my class had studied recorder and many of the students learned what C and G major scales were. We were able to use and understand words like *key*, *pitches*, and *steps*. Guitar began shortly after and learners were working at their own pace but we all at least got comfortable with the chords Em, C, and G. They were introduced to or had some experience with the chords D, Am, and F and most learned the first three to five notes of the C major scale. They had played a few chord progressions, and a few simple melodies. Near the end of the guitar unit, I showed them Axis of Awesome's video called "Four Chords." If you are unfamiliar with this video, I will explain:

Axis of Awesome is a comedy band and "Four Chords" is a song that they wrote which is a medley of over 50 songs all with the exact same chord progression. It gives you a great jumping off point for talking about composition and songwriting. Make sure you use the *clean* version of the song as the original has swear words in it. This song can easily be found on YouTube.

After they saw the video I explained to them that most songs only use four chords. I used the *Major Scale Chords* chart from the last chapter to help them understand what a *I–V–vi–IV* progression was and how we can transpose it to other keys and the pattern still stays the same. Axis of Awesome's song is in the key of D. Then I checked to see if they could find the progression on the chart. For this project, it is important that learners already understand the *Major Scale Chords* chart.

My plan that year was to have learners begin to write their own songs starting in March to perform in the spring concert in June. Our spring concert includes students in Grades 4–6. After they learned a few chords from the guitar unit and already understood what *key* meant from the recorder unit and their previous work with solfege, I thought it was a perfect time to begin writing their own songs. The concert ended up consisting of 50% original material. The rock band had already written their own songs and added them to the show. What art form other than music presents a show with 100% reproduced works? I can't think of any. Music is creative, but many times it is not being taught in a way that stimulates this creative aspect.

My Process
Chord Progressions

As you can tell from the *Major Scale Chords* chart in the previous chapter, and what I have already presented, the students were already familiar with the I(C), iii(Em), IV(F), V(G), and vi(Am) chords in the key of C as well as the I(G), ii(Am), IV(C), V(D), vi(Em) and $\flat VII$(F) chords in the key of G. Also, knowing from watching "Four Chords" that most songs in the world use only four chords the learners possessed the knowledge and skills they needed to write a chord progression of their own in either C or G. I thought since we were just on the tail end of our guitar unit that chord progressions would be the best place to start since those concepts were the freshest in their minds. We began by writing our own chord progression as a class using the *Major Scale Chords* chart. I asked the students to pick a key between C or G explaining that we know most of the chords in those keys. I also touched on the concept of the $\flat VII$ chords. Once key was established, I told them that if we are in C, we must have a C chord in it somewhere. The root chord is usually at the beginning or the end of the progression but I never told them where it had to be because I wanted them to get their creative juices flowing.

NOTE: In the previous chapter, I mentioned that key is not important in the composing process and to just let it happen. In this instance, many learners already understood the concept of key from their experience with recorder, so to reinforce this learning I wanted them to make sure they established a *key*. Since they were working in major keys and could only pick between two, many sounded the same which was very beneficial for the end piece. Stay tuned!

To demonstrate, as a class we picked three or four chords and put them in order, then I played it for them as they listened to see if they needed to change something or keep it. Here is an example of how we wrote it on the board and how I taught them to write theirs during their composition process:

Chord Progression Examples

Steve Giddings

C   Am   F   G

Idea 1 (in C)

C   C   G   F

Idea 2 (in C)

G   G   D   C

Idea 3 (in G)

NOTE: This is easy for them to understand but if your learners have a way to write it down that is clear and helps them remember their song, I say let it happen. Otherwise, the physical writing could get in the way of the creative process.

Many would be able to tell if something was off about the progression and want to change something. They know more than we think because they are constantly listening to the music all around them. It's engrained in their DNA. My words of wisdom as they were composing were: If it sounds good, it's probably good. Adversely, if it sounds bad it's probably—you guessed it—bad! Or, from the words of pop music instructors at the Rottertam Academy for Music Education, "Everything that you think sounds good *is* good. Your own ears are the only essential criteria. There are no other musical rules."[17] After our mini-lesson, I sent learners on their way to find a chord progression of their own. They were also told to write everything down. I gave them each the *Major Scale Chords* chart and some blank staff paper. Many did not use the staff paper, likely because their way of writing it down made sense to them. Some of the more advanced learners knew enough chords or had enough work ethic to try other keys.

Chord Progression Flow Chart

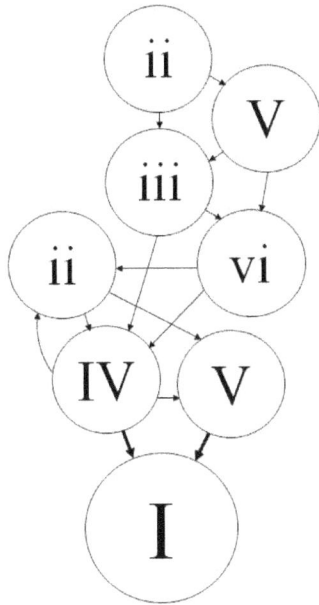

The Flow Chart

I used this flow chart (see *Chord Progression Flow Chart*) to help students find ideas for their chord progressions if they were completely stuck. I did one mini-lesson on it. To use this chart, you first need to decide if your progression starts on *I* or another chord. If it starts on *I*, begin with that, then jump anywhere else on the chart you would like. After this, follow the arrows. If you don't want it to start on *I*, then start wherever you would like and then follow the arrows. This chart will guarantee a good sounding chord progression but many are not overly interesting. Versions of this same flow chart can be found all over the internet. My version came from a combination of those charts found online.

For a couple of groups, as a way to help with writer's block, I introduced them to chord extensions. I showed them an example of what I meant. I started with a standard progression of C, Am, F, G and then added extensions to a couple of them to change the feel to something like CM^7, Am^7, F, G^7 and then played them the change. Some students really liked the change while others were unimpressed! I showed them a couple of books that have all the extensions possible on guitar in case they wanted to try a few. Many extensions can be found online using a quick Google search or by adding or taking away a finger in any chord form.

Melodies

After I felt that students had a handle on chord progressions and what they look and sound like, we started to experiment with melodies to go along with our chord progressions. Many knew that if their song was in G, they needed an F# instead of an F. I also found that many were confused about what a melody actually was. I had done an entire lesson on composing a melody and assumed they knew what I meant. They had even played plenty of melodies on recorder and guitar earlier and were still confused. The next class I had to take a step back and rework how I presented it. I asked them "How would you explain what a melody is to someone who knew absolutely nothing about music?" I got a range of answers from "it is how the song goes" to "melodies are one note at a time." Clearly, those students understood but had a hard time really putting it to words. We eventually agreed that melody was the part of the song that is sung or the *tune* of the song.

After that was established, I had a volunteer come up to the front of the class with an Orff mallet instrument. I asked another student in the class if we could use their chord progression. They gave me a chord progression that was in the key of C, we wrote it on the board and I instructed the learner on the Orff instrument to play along with me. Instead of improvising a melody, they often began playing the root notes of the chords that we wrote on the board. Many couldn't seem to separate the chords from the melody even though we have done plenty of jamming in this fashion on recorder. I told them to ignore the chords on the board and to make something up, and we started to get somewhere. I then invited the volunteer to pick three to five pitches from the scale and repeat them in a pattern. When they tried this, the learner began to compose a really catchy song. This seemed to click with many learners in the class so I told them that they were able to use one of the following instruments to come up with a melody for their song: their voice, an Orff mallet instrument, a guitar, a recorder, or a piano/keyboard. Many times during these melody writing sessions, I would go around with my guitar and play their chord progressions for them so they could hear their melodies with their chords. Many would use standard notation to write their melodies, others used an improvised form of tablature, while still others used more unconventional methods to write out their melodies. They just needed to be able to write it down somehow so that they could remember it. As mentioned earlier, forcing a particular form of notation will hinder the creative process.

After a couple of sessions of writing melodies, some students were migrating into their own groups and writing songs together. By the third time, I told them that if they wanted, they could get into groups to start composing together, and that they didn't need to start writing a new song if they decided to go with a partner, they could simply help their partner with a new part of their song. I found that many would take this approach and then settle on a song between them that they wanted to take to the next level. A lot of the time, since many of their songs were in the same key, they found that one learner's melody would go together with another learner's chord progression quite nicely.

Lyrics

When it comes to lyrics, I never know where to start. I find it difficult to come up with the right words in a poetic way. Many learners seem to have a bit of a knack with words and can write lyrics to songs quite easily. For those who don't have this seemingly magical skill, there are word webs.

I did a mini-lesson using a word web to write a verse of a song to show how to use it. The word web that I used had the topic box at the top and then two boxes extending from that. One was a *feeling* associated with the topic and the other was a *fact*. From there, we came up with words or small phrases that would come from the word before it until we felt we had enough or filled the page. Depending on the group, our songs ranged from being about how much we hate Transformers to having a best friend who can't dance and finding out later that it's SpongeBob SquarePants.

The Word Web

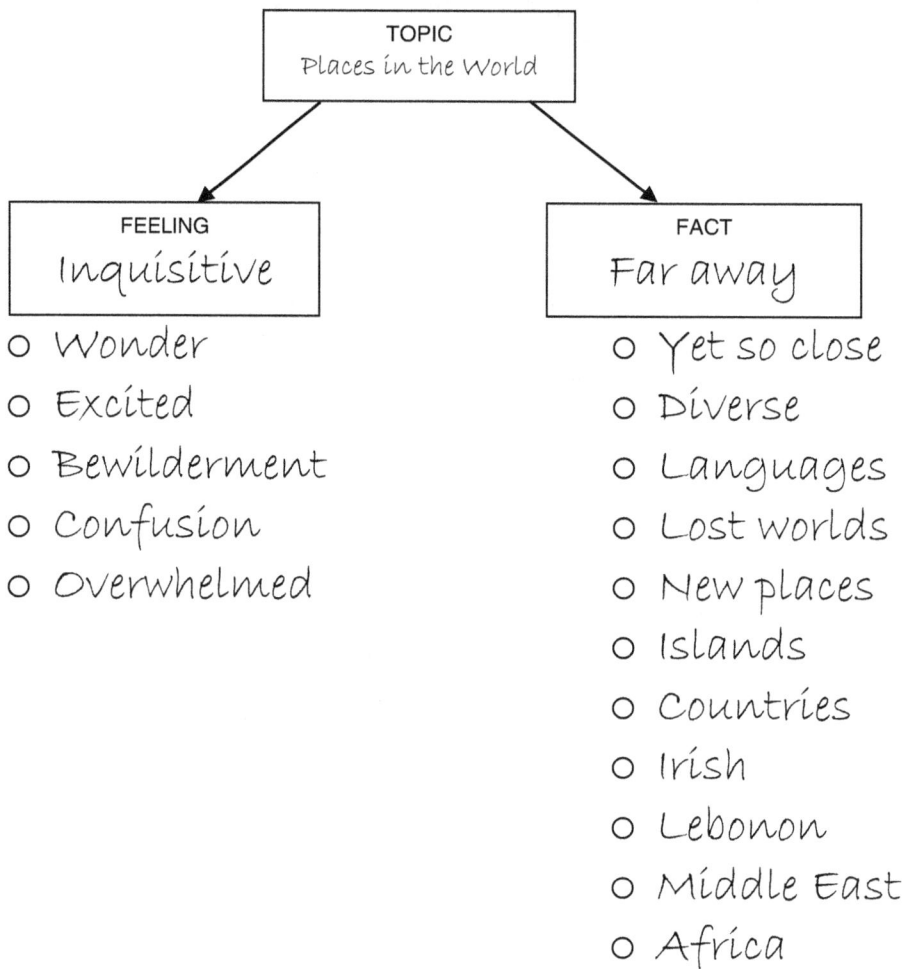

TOPIC
Places in the World

FEELING
Inquisitive

o Wonder
o Excited
o Bewilderment
o Confusion
o Overwhelmed

FACT
Far away

o Yet so close
o Diverse
o Languages
o Lost worlds
o New places
o Islands
o Countries
o Irish
o Lebonon
o Middle East
o Africa

Having lyrics first can sometimes help with writing a melody. Some students had a bit of a melody before writing their lyrics but when they started coming up with lyrics, their melody changed drastically to fit the words of the song. There is nothing wrong with this. It's all part of the process and learning how to write a song.

End Goal

Near the end of the project learners were forming into groups and some were wanting to write a song as a whole class. We ended up going with the whole class approach because there were smaller groups or individuals with many different snippets of a song already composed. Because many of them were in the same key, combining these snippets into one larger piece of music was incredibly easy.

To figure out what parts fit together or flowed well into one another we first had everyone perform what they had for the class. Most only had a chord progression or a short melody. Some had entire songs figured out. It is important here that learners know that even if they don't have an entire song, it's okay. It's the process that counts, and no contribution however small or large should be given priority over another. Then, as a class we chose which melodies, progressions, or song snippets we liked the best. Only a few classes with strong song writers were able to come up with lyrics on the spot or at home like in rock band rehearsals. Most classes had trouble with lyrics and melody so we had to use the word web as a class to come up with lyrics that fit our song. However, before we could add lyrics we had to make sure the form was completely composed and arranged. There were a range of processes that went on during this and every single one got the same end product—a song written together as a class.

In a High School Setting**

A rock ensemble can work really well in a high school setting. Of course, it could be an extracurricular ensemble but it could also be a course that is scheduled into the regular day as an option for any student to take. I published a version of the following outline in my 2008 article, but here is the updated course outline as I imagine it could look in a high school:

** A version of the following course outline was previously published in the Canadian Music Educator volume 49, issue 3, pp. 31–34.

Popular Music Performance Course Outline

Prerequisite: At least two years of private or group instruction on primary instrument or by audition.

Vision and Introduction

Throughout this course, students will be introduced to the real world skills and knowledge involved in becoming a professional musician. It will provide the learner with the tools to succeed in the field. The course will cover such topics as the by-ear-learning process, musical skills development, styles, and music technology. As well, every learner will have the opportunity to complete an independent project of their choice. This will give learners an opportunity to be a 'specialist' in their field. Assessment will be based on growth in one or more strands of the course. It will be an ongoing process that will allow the learner and coach to gain from each other and grow in a portion of the course.

Course Strands

Performance

> **a) Styles**: In small combos, students will display musicianship in *at least* four (4) different styles of popular music. This will be evaluated over a series of three to four performances which are organized throughout the semester/year.
>
> Ex: classic rock, metal, punk, 60s rock, 80s rock, or a combination of at least four others.
>
> **NOTE:** All groups must produce at least one fully composed original song per semester. More will be encouraged.
>
> **b) Technique**
>
> **Drummers**: Will be challenged with rudiments, improvisation, limb independence, and rhythm reading.
> **NOTE:** The *counting system* of rhythm works really well with drummers. An example of this would be "1 and 2 and 3 and 4 and."
> **Guitarists**: Will be challenged with scales, chords, improvisation, and songwriting.

Bassists: Will be challenged with scales, hand position, improvisation, and slap bass techniques.

Keyboardists: Will be challenged with scales, chords, improvisation, and lead sheet reading.

Vocalists: Will develop vocal techniques appropriate for various styles, growls, improvisation, and back up vocal techniques.

Horn Players: Will be challenged with by-ear-learning (as many horn players tend to be classically trained), scales, stylistically appropriate playing techniques, and improvisation.

Learners will be encouraged to examine a secondary or tertiary instrument. This happens naturally in rock music and should not be discouraged. This is not about switching instruments, it's about learning the basics of an additional instrument to help each musician understand one another on a deeper level.

Suggested Secondary Instruments:

Drummers: Rhythm guitar or bass
Lead Guitarist: Bass or lead vocals
Rhythm Guitarist: Bass or drums
Bassist: Drums or lead guitar
Vocalists: Guitar, drums, or keyboards
Keyboardists: Guitar or bass
Horn Players: Guitar or drums

> ***NOTE:*** Students can learn any other instrument they choose, these are just suggestions.

Musical Literacy

> **a) Aural Skills/Lifting**: Students will be expected to *lift* a number of tunes throughout the course to learn their music for each performance. They should be encouraged to rely on their ears primarily without using tablature or any other form of notation. This will help to develop the students' ear and become accustomed to some chord progressions or melodic motifs in rock music.

> **b) Theory:** Students will be expected to become fluent performers using *functional language* used by contemporary musicians. As well, each

instrumentalist will be encouraged to understand rhythm and notation as it applies to their particular instrument:

> **Guitar and Bass:** Challenged to understand rhythm and theory as it pertains to tablature and basic chord structure. For example, becoming familiar with the Nashville Number System would be extremely appropriate knowledge.

> **Keyboards:** Challenged to understand rhythm, basic triad and chord structure as it pertains to lead sheets. Becoming familiar with the Nashville Number System will be highly encouraged.

> **Vocals:** Challenged to understand solfa and sight-singing simple melodies.

> **Drums:** Challenged to understand rhythm notation and the *counting system* (1 and 2 and 3 and 4 and).

Technology

Learners will be introduced to standard recording equipment and performance technologies such as microphones, PA systems, micing and wiring techniques, and sound editing programs. Students will be expected to record themselves as a group for assessment purposes and individually for a recording project. They will pick at least one song to record and record it like professional studio musicians to produce a very high quality digital recording to present.

Independent Project:

The independent project can be done individually or in a group and can explore any one of the course strands covered in the course. The project should challenge the learner and must be approved via a written proposal. Suggestions will be available if a student cannot come up with an idea on their own. This project could range from learning modes to learning how to set up sound for a concert.

Assessment:

There will be two major assessment periods, and three if needed. The first is to give the learners and coach an idea of where the learners are coming from. The last is to show proof of growth in any one of the course strands. Learners will naturally demonstrate growth in all parts of the course but there will be at least one course strand where the learner shows the most growth. This may be assessed using rubrics on specific strands or a recording of the group to show ensemble and skills growth.

Break-down:

Performance: 40%
Musical Literacy: 20%
Technology: 20%
Independent Project: 20%

Some Considerations for This Course

Notation

To understand the Nashville Number System, learners must first understand scale degrees and basic rhythm notation. Also, musicians will not be required to understand traditional notation but should be at the very least introduced to the basics of traditional notation. They should understand its significance and be able to understand and write very simple melodies or, in the case of drummers, rhythm patterns. There **should not** be a focus on learning traditional notation but if a learner wants to explore this further with their independent project, this is completely fine.

I stress this because in a typical school setting, learning traditional notation is paramount and in many instances put before musicianship and listening skills. If not monitored closely, a classically trained teacher can easily stray into emphasizing traditional notation. This is neither an authentic nor useful way to learn rock music and can, many times, hinder the learning process.

Functional Language

Words like: *andante, crescendo, forte,* and other classical terms are irrelevant and not useful in rock music. Therefore, *functional language* refers to words that are used in rock music regularly such as: *chorus, verse, bridge, slower, faster, groove, louder, quieter,* and other such straightforward words. There is no need to complicate simple musical concepts by saying them in Italian. These traditional Italian musical terms are more appropriately learned in classical music as they are the *functional language* of musicians performing in that genre. Many times, in rock music, words do not even need to be exchanged if a group of musicians play well together or has lots of experience playing with other musicians—they can literally communicate to each other through the music itself. Some of this phenomenon is discussed in Chapter 6 (page 86). Also, when copying a song, the nuances are copied as well, making the use of descriptive musical terms not as useful.

Assessment

Assessment and testing can sometimes get in the way of quality learning. If it is done in such a way that it naturally highlights a learner's strengths or improvements then it won't. This is why demonstrating growth in at least one course strand ensures that every student will find success in their own way. Assessing growth can be difficult without records of where the learner came from. A good rock coach should know where a learner is coming from but learners don't always know or even think about it. This is why recording equipment is important and that every aspect of performance should be recorded at the beginning of the course. Some very short written pieces about their knowledge of concepts that cannot be captured by sound recordings would be appropriate as well. The second and third *snapshots*, whether they are audio or video, should show proof of growth in one or more strands of the course. This could be structured in such a way that learners must either demonstrate their new skills in a performance, a presentation of their new knowledge or a written report proving and arguing growth based on the collections of past and present recordings. As number or letter grades are usually necessary, each time they are assessed on their growth, a rubric gauging their level of growth in a particular strand will be provided.

This course, as much as possible, strays away from the *factory model* of education where everyone regardless of life experiences, skill level, or need is *assumed* to gain the exact same knowledge. The *factory model* ignores the fact that every learner is different and has different needs and interests not just as instrumentalists but as individuals. The *growth model* demonstrated here emphasizes the fact that every learner is different and will learn at their own pace and what is substantial growth for one learner may look completely different for another. It focuses on the autonomy of the learner which has been proven to enhance learner engagement.

Chapter 11: The Concert

You've made it this far and now it's time for your first performance with your young rockers. My concerts usually have the rock bands as the main ensemble throughout the show. I have done two main formats for my concerts in the past that showcase the rock groups and involve many other students as well:

Full-Fledged Concert Format

Our spring concerts include all extracurricular ensembles and all students from Grades 4–6. The bands perform every song they learned that year. This format is a favourite of mine because it gets everyone involved and lines up perfectly with the dance unit in the physical education department. The physical education teacher at my school choreographs simple dances to some of the band's songs and assigns a different one to each grade involved in the concert. Because there is a very prom-inent dance school in the community choreography is often learner-led. Not only will each class have a song to dance to, they will have a song to perform as a class that they learned through the *by-ear-learning process* from Chapter 10. The bands provide the music for the dances but also have their own feature songs that they perform. Recently, a concert we prepared was made up of 50% original works by students achieved by following the steps in the previous chapter. Each class wrote and per-formed their own songs and choreographed their own dances to a band tune. Here is a copy of the program from that concert:

The names of the bands that year were 2 K00L 4 SK00L and The Crickets and each night was slightly different with regard to what class was performing:

Tuesday, June 14, 2016

Separate Ways by Journey—2 K00L 4 SK00L
Keep Holding On by Avril Lavigne—Choreo by 4 C, music performed by 2 K00L 4 SK00L
Sing, Sing, Sing by Louis Prima—4 C
Juke Box Hero by Foreigner—2 K00L 4 SK00L
What You Need by INXS—Choreo by 5/6 P, music performed by 2 K00L 4 SK00L
Heavy Metal Chorus by 5/6 Power—Music written by 5/6 P
Down on the Corner by CCR—2 K00L 4 SK00L
Among the Stars by 2 K00L 4 SK00L—2 K00L 4 SK00L
Living on a Prayer by Bon Jovi—2 K00L 4 SK00L

Hello by Adele—Glee Choir
The Middle by Jimmy Eat World—Glee Choir
The Climb by Miley Cyrus—Glee Choir
Zip-a-dee-doo-dah from Alice and Wonderland—Glee Choir

House of the Rising Sun by The Animals—The Crickets
It's My Life by Bon Jovi—Choreo by 5 A, music performed by The Crickets
Time to Celebrate by 5 Arbuckle—Music written by 5 A
What About Love by Heart—The Crickets
Clocks by Coldplay—The Crickets
Take on Me by A-Ha—Choreo by 5/6 L, music performed by The Crickets
Get up and Dance by 5/6 Lawlor—Music written by 5/6 L
Enter Sandman by Metallica—The Crickets
Memories of the Past by The Crickets—The Crickets
Final Countdown by Europe—The Crickets

Wednesday, June 15, 2016

Separate Ways by Journey—2 K00L 4 SK00L
Keep Holding On by Avril Lavigne—Choreo by 4 S, music performed by 2 K00L 4 SK00L
Sing, Sing, Sing by Louis Prima—4 S
Juke Box Hero by Foreigner—2 K00L 4 SK00L
What You Need by INXS—Choreo by 6 S, music performed by 2 K00L 4 SK00L
Questions by 6 Shannon—Music written by 6 S
Down on the Corner by CCR—2 K00L 4 SK00L
Among the Stars by 2 K00L 4 SK00L—2 K00L 4 SK00L
Living on a Prayer by Bon Jovi—2 K00L 4 SK00L

The Ballad of the Bluenose by David D. Martins—2/3 Choir
Speak Life by TobyMac—2/3 Choir
Hello by Adele—Glee Choir
The Middle by Jimmy Eat World—Glee Choir
The Climb by Miley Cyrus—Glee Choir
Zip-a-dee-doo-dah from Alice and Wonderland—Glee Choir

House of the Rising Sun by The Animals—The Crickets
It's My Life by Bon Jovi—Choreo by 4/5 D, music performed by The Crickets
Stay With Me by 4/5 Dawn—Music written by 4/5 D
What About Love by Heart—The Crickets

Clocks by Coldplay—The Crickets
Take on Me by A-Ha—Choreo by 6 S, music performed by The Crickets
Um by 6 Sirois-Curtis—Music written by 6 S
Enter Sandman by Metallica—The Crickets
Memories of the Past by The Crickets—The Crickets
Final Countdown by Europe—The Crickets

Coffee House Format

This is a very relaxed style of concert where parents bring sweets for a bake sale during the show and tables with chairs and sometimes couches with coffee tables are set up instead of theatre style seating. People are free to mingle, eat, and listen to the music. It always features performances from the bands and other extracurricular ensembles and sometimes guest performing groups. Due to the seating format, this concert style is more conducive to smaller groups and a smaller number of students where there won't be hundreds of people in attendance.

Sound

Good sound is incredibly important in any show. It can turn a good performance into a great one or a great performance into a poor one. Chapter 3 discusses the basics of sound and how to choose the right PA system (see page 22). I learned about sound by doing it myself at school concerts. The kids led the performances, I did all the sound. There are many benefits to doing your own sound at a concert:

1. *Saves the school money:* renting equipment is very reasonable costing around $300 for everything you need for a basic setup.
2. *You are in control of the sound:* No one knows the band better than you do so you know exactly when to turn up the guitars for a solo and what part needs to come out more.
3. *Less stressful than playing with or conducting your learners:* If you are in charge of sound, that means that your learners are running the show. Therefore, you are not needed to conduct or play with your kids leading them to play with each other and learn valuable ensemble skills.

There are also some drawbacks to doing your own sound:

1. ***Setting up can be more time consuming.*** Typically, you are the only person in the school who will know how to set up the sound gear making it more time consuming than just plugging in a couple of microphones. Learners can be coached through the setup but that also takes time.
2. ***If something goes wrong with the sound during a concert, it can be quite stressful to try and fix it on the fly.*** With live sound, just the simple push of a single button can render the entire system temporarily useless or can cause an incredible amount of feedback.
3. ***If you are inexperienced, it can be more stressful.*** This does get better with time though, the more comfortable you get with the gear.

Hiring a sound company for your concert can be extremely beneficial as well:

1. ***It will be their job to fix any technical difficulties.*** Usually, there are no technical difficulties because the sound companies have training in live sound and have years of experience under their belts.
2. ***It causes zero added stress for you.*** They do all the work of set up and tear-down and all the live sound during the concert.

Of course, hiring a sound company comes with its drawbacks as well:

1. ***It can get expensive.*** Most professional sound companies charge between $800.00 and $1500.00 depending on how long you need them and how extensive the setup needs to be. Much, if not all of this, can be recouped by donations at the door however, but it can make an administrator weary about the initial upfront cost.
2. ***If a concert is postponed, they may not be available on that night.*** Some sound companies will anticipate this if it is a school concert but it is something to keep in mind.

Learner-Led

It is amazing how much learners can do with little or no help from their teacher. If your young musicians have been practicing how to set up their microphones and wrap their cables all year, and your guitar players have been practicing how to plug in and tune the guitars, your stress will be greatly reduced already because they will be able to handle a chunk of the setting up themselves. Older, more advanced students will be able to handle an entire sound setup on their own. Giving them this power teaches these learners valuable, practical musician skills that they will use.

As referenced earlier, seeing me conduct a choir or play with my rock group is extremely rare. I don't even address the audience very often. Only being at the mixer greatly reduces my stress and gives me a chance to actually sit back and enjoy the concert. Learners will rely on each other and *actually listen* to each other like real musicians instead of relying on me or watching my arms flail around up in front of them. I almost feel like a member of the audience because the learners are going through everything they need to on their own. Often, I will print off set lists for the band and put them in places where every musician can see the order. This way, they know exactly what to play next and can smoothly transition to the next song with few interruptions. These skills are practiced throughout the year so that, as their coach, you are not scrambling to teach them setup and transitions a week before the concert. By that point it should almost be automatic for them. Even with my youngest learners, I make sure they are always listening to how their performances sound so they can lead their own performances without me. By nature, my youngest learners do need more attention than my older ones, but the training for performance and musical independence begins in Kindergarten.

Conclusion

Throughout the course of this book, I took you on a journey from reasons to start a rock group, what gear you need, what songs to play, and how to be the best rock coach you can be through to the execution of your concert. With this knowledge and this book by your side you *will* be successful in coaching your very own rock band at your school. Learners under your supervision will experience music in an exciting and relevant way. They won't be forced to learn music they love outside of school and they will be given new opportunities to enjoy music in school while their learning complements all the amazing things already going on in your classroom. Rock bands are a relevant and sustainable way to teach music if taught in an authentic way that is true to the informal learning methods of rock musicians. This means the teacher is the facilitator or coach and all or most activities are learner-led, by-ear-learning based, and creativity based. If taught in the traditional manner of relying on notation, teacher-directed, and little or no *true* listening it will be ineffective, untrue, and musically hindering. However, if there is one take-away from this book, it is to **trust your learners as they know more than you think they do. Don't stress about knowing everything and don't be afraid to learn with your young rockers.** This book doesn't have all the answers but hopefully has answered many of your questions and calmed many of your concerns about teaching rock ensembles. In addition, if you are a seasoned rock coach, I hope you found something in this book to enhance your practice or found some inspiration within the pages. Keep in touch with my website and blog (stevesmusicroom.com) to help you along with teaching rock groups and check out my other articles on this topic and creativity too. I would love to hear your thoughts or just to hear about your successes with teaching rock groups. Please feel free to e-mail me any time at steve@stevesmusicroom.com.

You focus on being the kids' coach, let me focus on being yours!

References

1. Steve Giddings. "Why Our Work Matters." *Canadian Music Educator* 58, no. 1 (2016): 42–43.

2. Steve Giddings. "Popular Music Education: A Different Type of Musicianship; the follow-up." *Canadian Music Educator* 52, no. 2 (2010): 33–36.

3. Lev S. Vygotsky. *Mind in Society: The Development of Higher Psychological Processes.* Edited by Michael Cole, Vera John-Steiner, Sylvia Scribner and Ellen Souberman. (Cambridge, Massachusetts: Harvard University Press, 1978).

4. Lucy Green. *Music, Informal Learning and the School: A New Classroom Pedagogy.* (England: Ashgate Publishing Limited, 2008).

5. Robert H. Woody. "Playing by Ear: Foundation or Frill?" *Music Educators Journal* 99, no. 2 (2012): 82–88.

6. Lucy Green. *How Popular Musicians Learn: A Way Forward for Music Education.* (England: Ashgate Publishing Limited, 2002)

7. Woody, 83.

8. KG Johansson. "What Chord was That? A Study of Strategies Among Ear Players in Rock Music." In *Music, Education and Innovation*, edited by Cecelia Ferm Thorgersen and Karlsen Sidsel, 17–28. Pitea: Lulea University of Technology Press (2010).

9. Lucy Green. "Musical "Learning Styles" and "Learning Strategies" in the Isntrumental Lesson: Some Emergent Findings From a Pilot Study." *Psychology of Music* November (2010): 42–65.

10. Lars Lilliestam. "On Playing by Ear." *Popular Music* 15, no. 2 (May 1996): 195–216.

11. Angela Frucci. "MUSIC: Log On, Learn to Play (Without Reading a Note)." *The New York Times*, October 8, 2006.

12. Douglas E. Thompson. "Speaking Their Language: Guitar Tablature in the Middle School Classroom." *General Music Today* (2011): 53–57.

13. Mayne Smith. "A Shuffle in Charlie: Technical Communications Among Improvising Musicians (version 2.1)." *maynesmith.com*. April 23, 2010. http://maynesmith.com/pdfs/Shuffle%20in%20Charlie.pdf (accessed April 14, 2014).

14. Steve Giddings. "Inherent Creativity and the Road to Happiness." *Canadian Music Educator* 55, no. 2 (2013): 44–46.

15. *Ken Robinson: How Schools Kill Creativity*. TEDTalks Education: TED Conferences LLC. June 26, 2006.

16. Bill Dobbins. "Improvisation: An Essential Element of Musical Proficiency." *Music Educators Journal* 66, no. 5 (January 1980): 36–41.

17. Evelein Frits. "Pop and World Music in Dutch Music Education: Two Cases of Authentic Learning in Music Teacher Education and Secondary Music Education." *International Journal of Music Education* (2006): 178–187.